Symbol	Ingredient	Symbol	Ingredient	Symbol	Ingredient
	Irish whiskey				
	Islay single-malt Scotch				
	Kahlúa		Fresh orange juice		Simple syrup
	Kümmel		Orgeat syrup		Sloe gin
	Lemonade		Fresh passion fruit juice		Soda water
	Fresh lemon juice		Peach purée		Sugar cube
	Lemon-lime soda		Peychaud's Bitters		Tomato juice
	Light rum		Pimm's No. 1		Turbinado sugar
	Lillet Blonde		Fresh pineapple juice		Vermouth (dry)
	Fresh lime juice		Pisco		Vermouth (sweet)
	Madeira		Prosecco		Vodka
	Manzanilla sherry		Raspberry syrup		Water (spring or purified)
	Maraschino liqueur		Ruby port		White crème de cacao
	Mint		Rye		White rum
	Orange bitters		Scotch (12 years old)		Whole milk
	Orange blossom water		Scotch/Blended Scotch whiskey		Wine (sparkling/ dry sparkling)
	Orange curaçao		Silver tequila		Worcestershire sauce

S

THE ARCHITECTURE
of the
COCKTAIL

Constructing the Perfect Cocktail from the Bottom Up

WRITTEN BY AMY ZAVATTO – ILLUSTRATIONS BY MELISSA WOOD

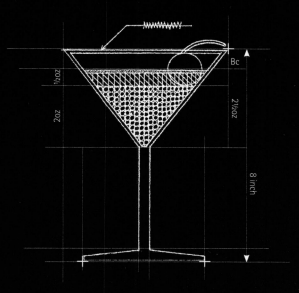

Race Point
PUBLISHING

Race Point
PUBLISHING

A division of Book Sales, Inc.
276 Fifth Avenue, Suite 206
New York, New York 10001

RACE POINT PUBLISHING and the distinctive Race Point Publishing logo
are trademarks of Book Sales, Inc.

© 2013 by Race Point Publishing
Illustrations © Melissa Wood 2013

ISBN-13: 978-1-937994-32-7

Printed in China

2 4 6 8 10 9 7 5 3 1

www.racepointpub.com

MIXING SYMBOLS

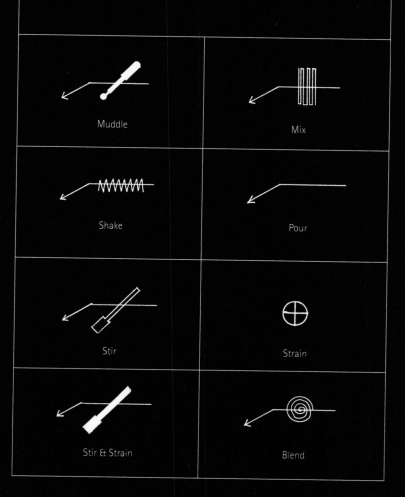

Muddle

Mix

Shake

Pour

Stir

Strain

Stir & Strain

Blend

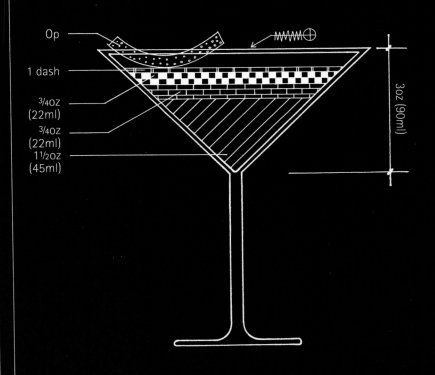

Op

1 dash

3/4oz
(22ml)

3/4oz
(22ml)

1½oz
(45ml)

3oz (90ml)

SPECIFICATIONS		EMBELLISHMENTS
Gin	Fresh orange juice	Orange peel (Op)
Lillet Blonde	Orange bitters	

ABBEY

While the raw materials of the Abbey are certainly the good stock of a well-constructed cocktail, it's this drink's orange-hued elegance that draws you in immediately. Like an aesthetically pleasing building, statue, or park, you are first taken in by the beauty of the sum of its parts. Ah, but what good parts it has! The Abbey is a genteel tipple, using the whisperingly sweet French-wine-based aperitif Lillet to highlight and support the botanicals in its main spirit, gin, as well as the bright and bitter accent of the orange bitters. The drink made its first appearance in the venerable *Savoy Cocktail Book*, circa 1930, and while it has not garnered the fame of other, more well-known cocktails, this nearly forgotten, refreshing tipple is more than worth taking a moment to discover and admire.

THE NOTES

Place 6 or 7 square ice cubes into a cocktail shaker. Pour in 1½ fluid ounces (45ml) of gin, coating the ice. Add in ¾ fluid ounce (22ml) of Lillet Blonde, ¾ fluid ounce (22ml) of fresh orange juice, and 1 dash of orange bitters. Shake in a vertical motion for 30 seconds. Strain slowly into a cocktail glass. Using a channel knife or standard vegetable peeler, gently slice only the skin (avoiding the bitter pith) of an orange above the drink and drop the peel into the glass.

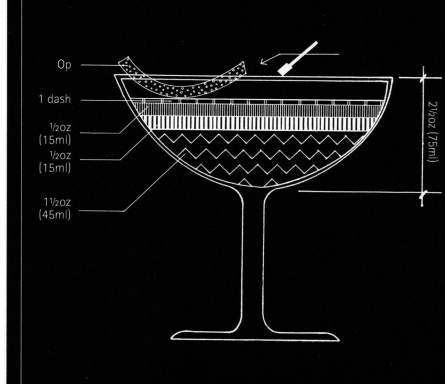

Op

1 dash

1/2oz
(15ml)

1/2oz
(15ml)

11/2oz
(45ml)

2 1/2oz (75ml)

	SPECIFICATIONS		EMBELLISHMENTS
	Fino sherry	Dry vermouth	Orange peel (Op)
	Sweet vermouth	Orange bitters	

| 6 | ADONIS |

ADONIS

To simply send a person out on a mission to get sherry for the classic tipple the Adonis is like asking a carpenter to go out to buy some wood to make a floor. Should it be oak? Teak? Cherry? Which kind? You need to specify or you'll get something entirely different from what you envisioned. Sherry, as you may well know, can range in flavor from lip-smackingly dry, to nutty and mild, to rich and sweet. In the case of the Adonis, you want to lean toward the drier side of sipping and opt for a light, dry fino sherry, as this cocktail is best when served as a sophisticated, light predinner aperitif.

THE NOTES

Place 6 or 7 square ice cubes into a cocktail shaker. Pour in 1½ fluid ounces (45ml) of fino sherry, coating the ice. Add in ½ fluid ounce (15ml) each of dry and sweet vermouth and 1 dash of orange bitters. Using a long bar spoon, quickly stir the cocktail's ingredients for 30 seconds. Strain slowly into a coupe glass. Using a channel knife or standard vegetable peeler, gently slice only the skin (avoiding the bitter pith) of an orange above the drink and drop the peel into the glass.

ALLEGHENY

If you build it, they will come—more or less—that's the loose history of the Allegheny cocktail in a nutshell. Or, perhaps, in a whiskey still. The name itself comes from the chain of peaks that is part of the Appalachian mountain chain in America, and supposedly the drink was made to honor the hardscrabble pioneers who crossed that range and settled the state of Kentucky—and apparently founded the ironically dry Bourbon County, where corn whiskey moonshine was distilled in the quiet of the thick Appalachian woods. A good story certainly makes for a great creation, but what's truly lovely about this drink is the way the rich, ripe, fruity flavor of the blackberry brandy teases out the vanilla notes and dark baking-spice flavors in the bourbon whiskey.

THE NOTES

Place 6 or 7 square ice cubes into a cocktail shaker. Pour in 1 fluid ounce (30ml) of bourbon whiskey, coating the ice. Add ½ fluid ounce (15ml) of blackberry brandy, then 1 fluid ounce (30ml) of dry vermouth and the fresh juice of ½ a lemon. Shake in a vertical motion for 30 seconds. Strain slowly into a cocktail glass. Using a channel knife or standard vegetable peeler, gently slice only the skin (avoiding the bitter pith) of a lemon above the drink and drop the peel into a glass.

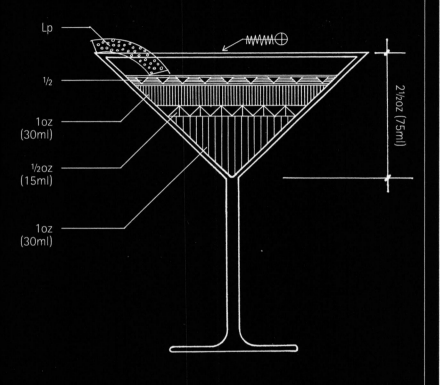

Lp

½

1oz
(30ml)

½oz
(15ml)

1oz
(30ml)

2½oz (75ml)

SPECIFICATIONS		EMBELLISHMENTS	
Bourbon whiskey	Dry vermouth		
Blackberry brandy	Fresh lemon juice	Lemon peel (Lp)	

ALLEGHENY | 9

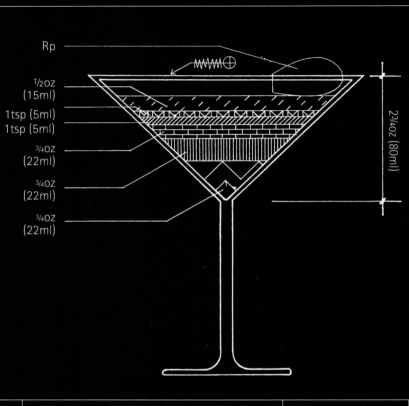

Rp

1/2 OZ
(15ml)

1 tsp (5ml)
1 tsp (5ml)

3/4 OZ
(22ml)

3/4 OZ
(22ml)

3/4 OZ
(22ml)

2 3/4 oz (80ml)

	SPECIFICATIONS		EMBELLISHMENTS
	Brandy	Grenadine	
	Dry vermouth	White crème de menthe	
	Fresh orange juice	Ruby port	Rose petal (Rp)

| 10 | AMERICAN BEAUTY |

AMERICAN BEAUTY

Sometimes nature is the best, most consistent architect of all. Consider the rose: its perfect multilayered construction is as unique and flawless as the swirl of the Guggenheim Museum on New York's Fifth Avenue. And as it so happens, Mother Nature is the inspiration behind the creation of this complex sipper, named for the pink-petaled rose. The combination of amber-hued brandy, yellowish dry vermouth, orange juice, vibrant grenadine, and white crème de menthe mix up a perfect blush of a cocktail, with a dribbled float of rich ruby port on top to add extra color saturation to this sippable eye candy.

THE NOTES

Place 6 or 7 square ice cubes into a cocktail shaker. Combine 3/4 fluid ounce (22ml) of brandy, 3/4 fluid ounce (22ml) of dry vermouth, and 3/4 fluid ounce (22ml) of fresh orange juice in the shaker with 1 teaspoon (5ml) of grenadine and 1 teaspoon (5ml) of white crème de menthe. Shake in a vertical motion for 30 seconds. Strain into a cocktail glass. Using a wide-mouthed spoon or small pitcher, slowly float 1/2 fluid ounce (15ml) of ruby port on top. Garnish with a rose petal.

AMERICANO

Originally called the Milan-Torino at Gaspare Campari's Turin-based bar, so many post-Prohibition-era American tourists appeared to order it by the bucketful, it became known as the Americano.

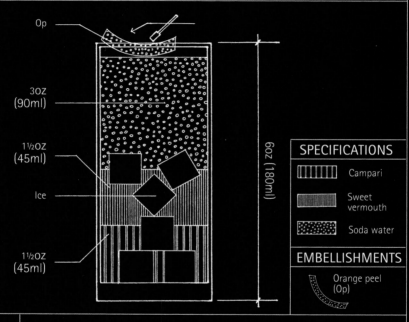

0p

3OZ (90ml)

1½OZ (45ml)

Ice

1½OZ (45ml)

6oz (180ml)

SPECIFICATIONS

▦	Campari
▦	Sweet vermouth
▦	Soda water

EMBELLISHMENTS

Orange peel (0p)

THE NOTES

Place 5 or 6 square ice cubes into a highball glass. Pour in 1½ fluid ounces (45ml) of Campari and 1½ fluid ounces (45ml) of sweet vermouth, allowing the two to mingle with the ice for a moment. Fill with 3 fluid ounces (90ml) of soda water and stir well with a long bar spoon, until all of the ingredients are fully mixed. Using a channel knife or standard vegetable peeler, gently slice only the skin (avoiding the bitter pith) of an orange above the drink and drop the peel into the glass.

ANGEL'S KISS

The beauty of this pre-Prohibition-era drink lies not in its delightfully romantic name, nor the notion that it is a perfect after-dinner indulgence if you have a sweet tooth—it's in the layering.

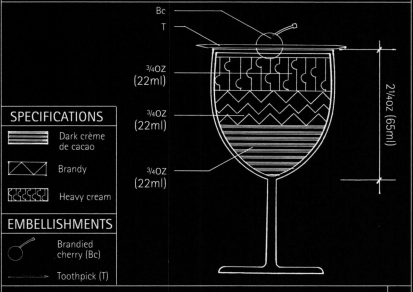

Bc
T

¾OZ (22ml)

¾OZ (22ml)

¾OZ (22ml)

2¼oz (65ml)

SPECIFICATIONS

Dark crème de cacao

Brandy

Heavy cream

EMBELLISHMENTS

Brandied cherry (Bc)

Toothpick (T)

THE NOTES

Pour ¾ fluid ounce (22ml) of heavy cream into a bowl and whip until frothy (but not until the cream becomes stiff). With the stem in your hand, flip over a teaspoon so that the rounded bottom is now pointing up. Hold the spoon just below the rim against the inside of a port glass and slowly pour ¾ fluid ounce (22ml) of dark crème de cacao (or your favorite chocolate liqueur) into the glass. Repeat this same technique with ¾ fluid ounce (22ml) of brandy and then the cream, making sure you just drizzle the last layer in order to achieve the trilayering needed for the final appearance. Pierce a brandied cherry with a long toothpick and place it so that each end is on one side of the glass, balanced over the cocktail.

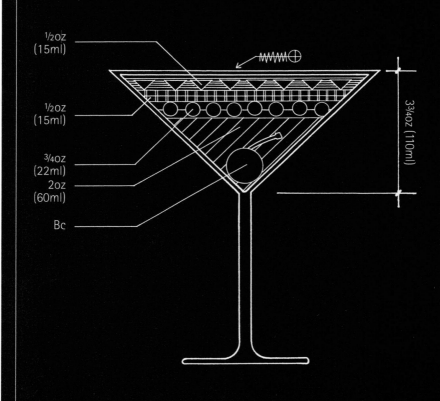

½oz
(15ml)

½oz
(15ml)

¾oz
(22ml)

2oz
(60ml)

Bc

3¾oz (110ml)

SPECIFICATIONS		EMBELLISHMENTS
Gin	Crème de violette	
Maraschino liqueur	Fresh lemon juice	Brandied cherry (Bc)

14   AVIATOR

AVIATOR

Can a cocktail take flight? The resurgence in wild popularity of this pre-Prohibition-era tipple certainly makes a good case for it. Find any cool cocktail bar that doesn't have this sipper on its list, and I can only surmise that they ran out of gin. Why did it fall from grace for so many dark decades? Blame the difficulty of bartenders in getting their hands on once-available ingredients like crème de violette and maraschino liqueur, the keys to its pretty hue and subtle undertones of sweetness. Bright, refreshing, and a little bit complex, this classic cocktail makes a great impression on houseguests who were expecting no more titillation than mere tonic.

THE NOTES

Drop a brandied cherry into the bottom of a cocktail glass. Set aside. Place 6 or 7 square ice cubes into a cocktail shaker. Pour in 2 fluid ounces (60ml) of gin, coating the ice. Add ¾ fluid ounce (22ml) of maraschino liqueur, ½ fluid ounce (15ml) of crème de violette, and ½ fluid ounce (15ml) of fresh lemon juice. Shake in a vertical motion for 30 seconds. Strain into the cocktail glass.

BELLINI

This drink was appropriately invented in the floating city of Venice at Harry's Bar by Giuseppe Cipriani, and while finding a vacant stool at Harry's to enjoy this Italian original may prove far more difficult than sipping such an easygoing classic, as long as you can open a bottle of sparkling wine, it is perhaps the simplest of cocktails to prepare at home.

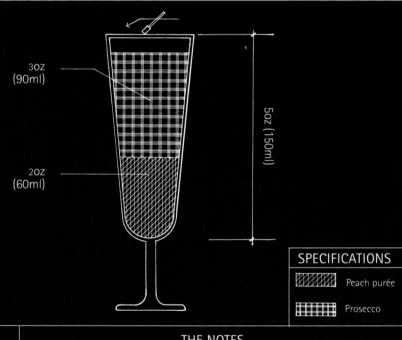

3OZ
(90ml)

2OZ
(60ml)

5oz (150ml)

SPECIFICATIONS

Peach purée

Prosecco

THE NOTES

Pour 2 fluid ounces (60ml) of peach purée into a champagne flute. Slowly pour in 3 fluid ounces (90ml) of prosecco, allowing the two ingredients to mix. Use a long bar spoon to carefully stir any purée that appears trapped at the bottom of the glass.

BIJOU

Bijou means "jewel" in French, and the interesting addition of green Chartreuse in this drink—combined with sweet red vermouth—creates a gem of an amber-hued sipper.

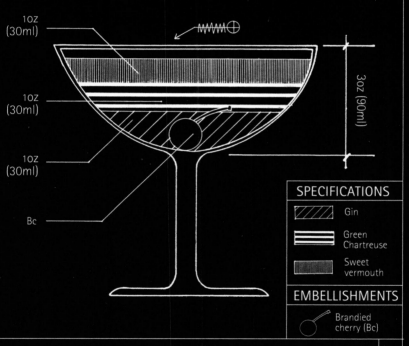

1OZ (30ml)

1OZ (30ml)

1OZ (30ml)

Bc

3oz (90ml)

SPECIFICATIONS

//////	Gin
≡≡≡	Green Chartreuse
▓▓▓	Sweet vermouth

EMBELLISHMENTS

Brandied cherry (Bc)

THE NOTES

Drop a brandied cherry into the bottom of a coupe glass. Set aside. Place 6 or 7 square ice cubes into a cocktail shaker. Pour in 1 fluid ounce (30ml) of gin, coating the ice. Add 1 fluid ounce (30ml) of green Chartreuse and 1 fluid ounce (30ml) of sweet vermouth. Shake in a vertical motion for 30 seconds. Strain into the coupe glass.

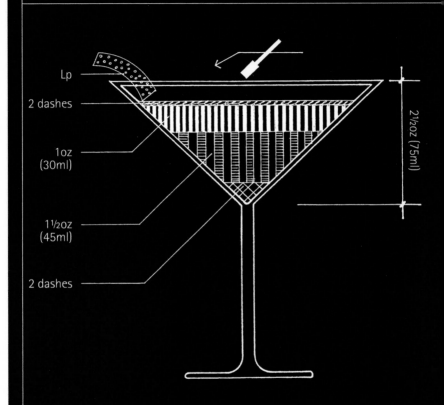

Lp

2 dashes

1oz
(30ml)

1½oz
(45ml)

2 dashes

2½oz (75ml)

SPECIFICATIONS		EMBELLISHMENTS
Absinthe	Dry vermouth	
Irish whiskey	Angostura bitters	Lemon peel (Lp)

18   BLACKTHORN

BLACKTHORN

Often good structure requires being open-minded—the ability to mingle myriad ideas, taking the best parts of them and bringing them into one glorious result. That's the Blackthorn. With the absinthe wash of a Sazerac, the inarguably perfect ingredients of a Manhattan (with sweet vermouth swapped for dry), plus the switch of soft and pleasing Irish whiskey for rye, this tipple makes for the sophisticated love child of all three. You may see some Blackthorn recipes that are entirely different from this, using sloe gin as the main ingredient, but I love the genius construction of this one.

THE NOTES

Pour 2 dashes of absinthe into a cocktail glass. Gently tip the glass and rotate, allowing the absinthe to coat the inside. Set aside. Place 6 or 7 square ice cubes into a cocktail shaker. Pour in 1½ fluid ounces (45ml) of Irish whiskey, coating the ice. Add 1 fluid ounce (30ml) of dry vermouth and 2 dashes of Angostura bitters. Using a long bar spoon, quickly stir the cocktail's ingredients for 30 seconds. Strain slowly into the cocktail glass. Using a channel knife or standard vegetable peeler, gently slice only the skin (avoiding the bitter pith) of a lemon above the drink and drop the peel into the glass.

BLOOD AND SAND

Some materials have a hard time breaking out of their workhorse status. Like, say, concrete—known as the source of sturdy foundations but never used for beauty until a few genius craftsmen figured out that it makes a sturdy, eco-friendly material for counters, floors, and other aesthetic visuals of value. Scotch is a little like this, too. Long sequestered to fireside drams with, perhaps, a touch of water or an ice cube, its merits have been long extolled, but it's not often elevated beyond its neat-in-the-glass functionality to high-cocktail status. That's why cocktails like the Blood and Sand are entirely necessary. Blended scotch (yes, even certain single malts) makes for a gorgeous cocktail base, and this is a great example of how it plays well with others. One caveat: although Islay malts can make for some really interesting cocktails (thank the popularity of smoky mezcal and creative modern bartenders for that!), a robust but honeylike Highland malt makes for a better complement here.

THE NOTES

Place 6 or 7 square ice cubes into a cocktail shaker. Pour in ¾ fluid ounce (22ml) of Scotch, coating the ice. Add in ¾ fluid ounce (22ml) of sweet vermouth, ¾ fluid ounce (22ml) of Cherry Heering, and ¾ fluid ounce (22ml) of fresh orange juice. Shake in a vertical motion for 30 seconds. Strain slowly into a coupe glass. Using a channel knife or standard vegetable peeler, gently slice only the skin (avoiding the bitter pith) of an orange above the drink and drop the peel into the glass.

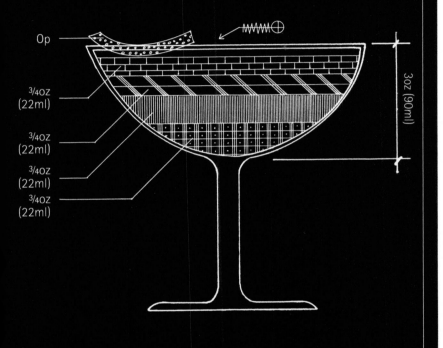

Op

³/₄OZ
(22ml)

³/₄OZ
(22ml)

³/₄OZ
(22ml)

³/₄OZ
(22ml)

3oz (90ml)

SPECIFICATIONS

Scotch

Cherry Heering

Sweet vermouth

Fresh orange juice

EMBELLISHMENTS

Orange peel
(Op)

BLOOD AND SAND | 21

BLOODY MARY

The indisputable king of classic brunch drinks, the Bloody Mary is a case study in the importance of getting your measurements just right. Some drinks—like a gin and tonic, for instance—certainly owe their echelons of excellence to the use of good ingredients, but if the measurements are off a little? The drink isn't bad—it's, perhaps, a little boozier or sweeter than you'd like, but as long as you're using quality gin and quality tonic, it still tastes pretty darned good. But adding too much or too little of an ingredient to a Bloody Mary? Disaster. If you've ever had a bad Bloody Mary (and I know you have), then you are nodding in agreement. A bad one can put you off the drink forever, amen. A good one, though? It will have you smacking your lips in anticipation of one of the most delicious savory cocktails there is to be sipped.

THE NOTES

Place 6 or 7 square ice cubes into a cocktail shaker. Pour in 2 fluid ounces (60ml) of vodka, coating the ice. Add 3 fluid ounces (90ml) of tomato juice, ½ teaspoon of grated horseradish, 2 dashes each of hot sauce and Worcestershire sauce, and ½ fluid ounce (15ml) of fresh lemon juice. Finish with ¼ teaspoon of coarse salt, ¼ teaspoon of black pepper, and ¼ teaspoon of celery salt. Shake in a vertical motion for 30 seconds. Strain slowly into an ice-filled Collins glass. Garnish with a lemon wedge and a celery stalk.

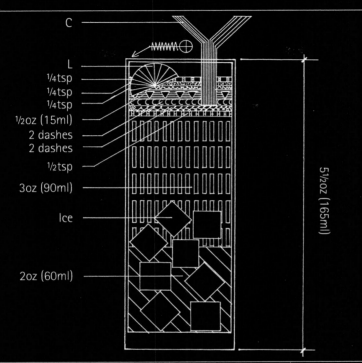

C

L

1/4 tsp
1/4 tsp
1/4 tsp

1/2 oz (15ml)
2 dashes
2 dashes

1/2 tsp

3oz (90ml)

Ice

2oz (60ml)

5 1/2 oz (165ml)

SPECIFICATIONS		EMB.
Vodka	Fresh lemon juice	Lemon wedge (L)
Tomato juice	Coarse salt	
Fresh grated horseradish	Cracked black pepper	Celery stalk (C)
Hot sauce	Celery salt	
Worcestershire sauce		

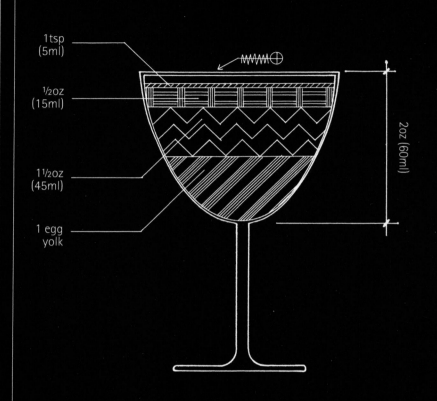

1tsp
(5ml)

½oz
(15ml)

1½oz
(45ml)

1 egg
yolk

2oz (60ml)

SPECIFICATIONS

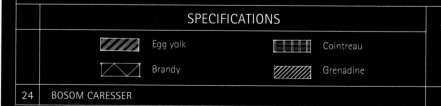

Egg yolk		Cointreau
Brandy		Grenadine

BOSOM CARESSER

One of the many wonderful results of the renaissance of classic cocktail culture the free world 'round is the long-lost discovery of cocktails that use egg as an ingredient. Eggs are a miraculous game changer in any recipe, be it fresh mayonnaise or a drink like this one, as the textural changes they add are nothing short of a little miracle. Whip or shake one hard enough and *poof*, you have something frothy, creamy, or velvety. And in the case of the Bosom Caresser, the egg is the solidifying, hold-it-together girder that makes the drink. As with any recipe that contains raw egg, remember to refrigerate your eggs as you normally would, removing them for use just prior to making the cocktail. And, of course, once it's made, don't walk away and leave it sitting out for an hour. Drink it!

THE NOTES

Place 6 or 7 square ice cubes into a cocktail shaker. Drop in the egg yolk, and then pour in 1½ fluid ounces (45ml) of brandy, ½ fluid ounce (15ml) of Cointreau, and 1 teaspoon (5ml) of grenadine. Shake in a vertical motion for 30 seconds. Strain slowly into a wineglass.

BRANDY ALEXANDER

Praised in song (who wouldn't want to be the subject of Canadian songstress Feist's boozy eponymous ballad?) and sipped with relish, the Brandy Alexander falls into that lovely, oft-forgotten category of dessert drinks. But dessert in a glass is a pleasure worth pursuing and doing correctly, especially when it comes to the use of heavy-lifter materials like cream. Adding the cream as one of the first ingredients to your shaker allows it to stay near icy cold, allowing maximum froth potential as the cream's molecules hold together like two securely nailed beams. What you get: a creamy, cold, gently sweet treat that, at first sip, is a little like taking your first step into new snow.

THE NOTES

Place 6 or 7 square ice cubes into a cocktail shaker. Pour in ¾ fluid ounce (22ml) of Scotch, coating the ice. Pour in 1 fluid ounce (30ml) of heavy cream, allowing it to coat the ice cubes. Add in 1 fluid ounce (30ml) of brandy and 1 fluid ounce (30ml) of white crème de cacao. Shake in a vertical motion for 30 seconds. Strain slowly into a cocktail glass. Grate fresh nutmeg over the top.

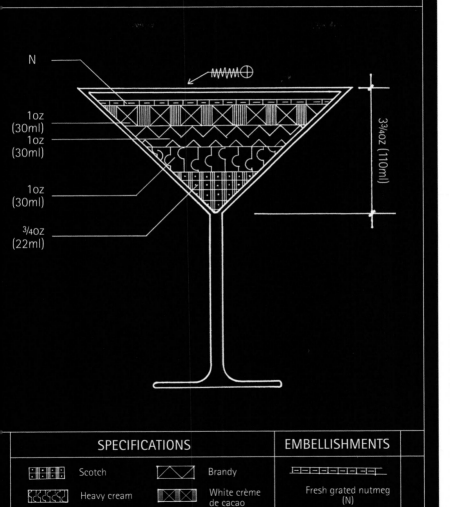

N

MWMW⊕

3¾oz (110ml)

1oz
(30ml)

1oz
(30ml)

1oz
(30ml)

¾OZ
(22ml)

SPECIFICATIONS		EMBELLISHMENTS
▦ Scotch	◹◺ Brandy	⊟⊟⊟⊟⊟⊟⊟⊟
⫟ Heavy cream	▨ White crème de cacao	Fresh grated nutmeg (N)

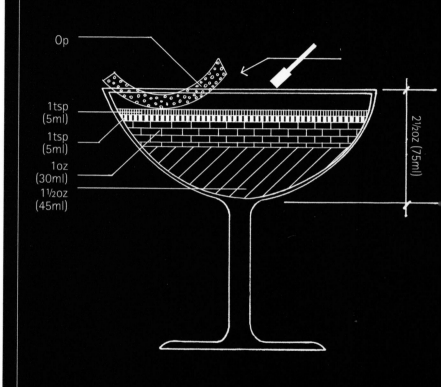

Op

1tsp
(5ml)

1tsp
(5ml)

1oz
(30ml)

1½oz
(45ml)

2½oz (75ml)

SPECIFICATIONS		EMBELLISHMENTS
Gin	Sweet vermouth	
Fresh orange juice	Dry vermouth	Orange peel (Op)

BRONX

Using the right *amount* of materials can be just as important as using the right materials when it comes to creating something. Take the Bronx cocktail, for instance. An argument could be made that this drink needs to be adjusted for the taste of the individual sipper, as—without the orange juice—it is basically a perfect martini, a drink whose proportions of vermouth, whether "dry" (very little vermouth) or "wet" (more vermouth), are continuously argued about. But the Bronx is meant to be a refreshing drink, and the addition of both sweet and dry vermouth in equal amounts is part of its fresh, flavorful charm.

THE NOTES

Place 6 or 7 square ice cubes into a cocktail shaker. Pour in 1½ fluid ounces (45ml) of gin, coating the ice. Add 1 fluid ounce (30ml) of fresh orange juice and 1 teaspoon (5ml) each of sweet and dry vermouth. Using a long bar spoon, stir for 30 seconds. Strain slowly into a coupe glass. Using a channel knife or standard vegetable peeler, gently slice only the skin (avoiding the bitter pith) of an orange above the drink and drop the peel into the glass.

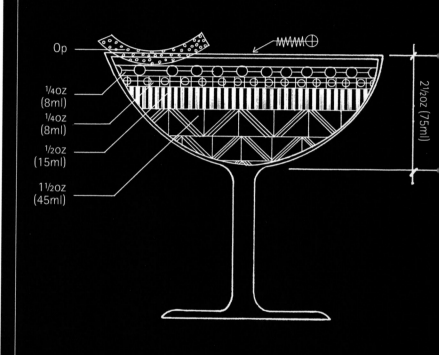

Op

2¹/₂oz (75ml)

¹/₄oz
(8ml)

¹/₄oz
(8ml)

¹/₂oz
(15ml)

1¹/₂oz
(45ml)

SPECIFICATIONS		EMBELLISHMENTS
Rye	Amer Picon	Orange peel (Op)
Dry vermouth	Maraschino liqueur	

BROOKLYN

You might argue that the rise in popularity of the County of Kings and the rise in popularity of the New York City borough's namesake tipple had a not entirely unparallel upward zoom in favor. Those who already loved them both knew their charms; but there were those who were uninitiated and needed convincing ("Why would *anyone* schlep out to Bushwick or for that matter mix rye and dry vermouth?!" could have easily once been the fictional decry). But just as Brooklyn has become the new black in popular NYC culture, so has its cocktail taken a sturdy spot on the lists of many a de rigueur bar. Why? The combination of spicy, snappy rye; dry, herby vermouth; and a gently bittersweet one-two punch of the once impossible to find Amer Picon (an Italian *amaro*) and maraschino liqueur adds a thought-provoking, entirely satisfying complexity to this king of a drink.

THE NOTES

Place 6 or 7 square ice cubes into a cocktail shaker. Pour in 1 ½ fluid ounces (45ml) of rye, coating the ice. Add in ½ fluid ounce (15ml) of dry vermouth, ¼ fluid ounce (8ml) of Amer Picon, and ¼ fluid ounce (8ml) maraschino liqueur. Shake in a vertical motion for 30 seconds. Strain slowly into a coupe glass. Using a standard vegetable peeler, gently slice only the skin (avoiding the bitter pith) of an orange above the drink and drop the peel in the glass.

CAIPIRINHA

Can a country have a national drink? In the case of beautiful Brazil, yes. The incredibly refreshing, simple genius of the Caipirinha (in loose phonetics, that's *keye-pir-een-ya*, if you're unsure how to ask a bartender for one) might also be considered the world's best drink on a hot summer's day, with its zippy burst of fresh lime juice and sweet kick of turbinado sugar and cachaça (*cuh-shah-suh*). What's cachaça, you ask? It's Brazil's very own rumlike spirit distilled from fermented sugarcane juice. If you can't find cachaça in your local liquor hub, don't worry. Simply substitute your favorite Russian vodka, and voilà, you have the Caipiroska—because geographical boundaries should never stop you from having a good drink.

THE NOTES

Cut a lime in half lengthwise. Set one of the halves aside. Slice the other half into four pieces. Place the pieces in a rocks glass and add 2 teaspoons (10ml) of turbinado sugar. Using a muddler or a sturdy wooden spoon, gently but thoroughly muddle the lime quarters and the sugar. Fill the glass with crushed ice and then pour in 2 fluid ounces (60ml) of cachaça. Stir gently for 5 seconds to allow the ingredients to properly blend. Slice off a wedge from the reserved half lime, make a small horizontal slice across its middle, and nestle onto the edge of the glass.

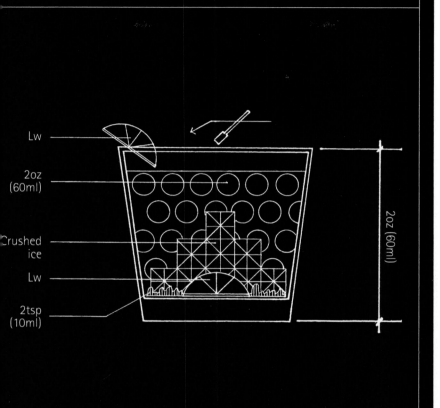

| Lw |
| 2oz (60ml) |
| Crushed ice |
| Lw |
| 2tsp (10ml) |

2oz (60ml)

SPECIFICATIONS

| ⊙ ⊙ ⊙ Cachaça | ▽▽▽ Fresh lime |
| Turbinado sugar | |

EMBELLISHMENTS

Lime wedge (Lw)

CAIPIRINHA | 33

CHRYSANTHEMUM

It's hard to say how or why some cocktails find their way back into the popular consciousness of the imbibing public, but if there were any drink ripe for a revival, I'd bet on the Chrysanthemum. First seen in print in the classic barkeep's bible *The Savoy Cocktail Book* of 1930, its ingredients—dry vermouth, Bénédictine, and absinthe—may well have been unwelcome in the collective cocktail culture only a decade ago. However, the rewelcoming of absinthe in the United States in 2007 combined with the rise in popularity of all things bitter and herby make this underdog of a classic a welcome return to the bars of today. It's also one of those drinks that manages to be simultaneously impressive and as easy as pie. And, come on, who doesn't want to drink something with such a lovely name?

THE NOTES

Place 6 or 7 square ice cubes into a cocktail shaker. Pour in 1½ fluid ounces (45ml) of dry vermouth, coating the ice. Add ¾ fluid ounce (22ml) of Bénédictine and 1 teaspoon (5ml) of absinthe. Using a long bar spoon, stir for 30 seconds. Strain slowly into a coupe glass. Using a channel knife or standard vegetable peeler, gently slice only the skin (avoiding the bitter pith) of an orange above the drink and drop the peel into the glass.

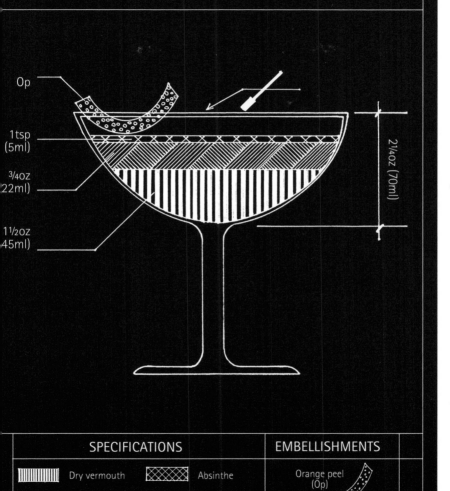

Op

1tsp
(5ml)

3/4oz
(22ml)

1 1/2oz
(45ml)

2 1/4oz (70ml)

SPECIFICATIONS		EMBELLISHMENTS	
▨ Dry vermouth ⊠ Absinthe		Orange peel (Op)	
▨ Bénédictine			
		CHRYSANTHEMUM	35

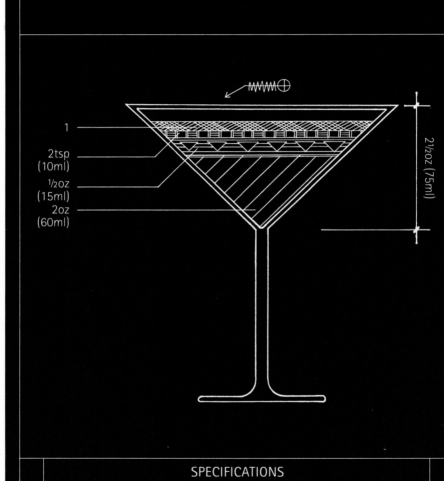

1

2tsp
(10ml)

½oz
(15ml)

2oz
(60ml)

2½oz (75ml)

SPECIFICATIONS

Gin		Raspberry syrup
Fresh lemon juice		Egg white

CLOVER CLUB

Do real men and women drink pink? If the cocktail in question is the Clover Club, they should. The drink's name is purported to have come from the pre-Prohibition eponymous Philadelphia, PA, men's club that used to meet in the Bellevue-Stratford Hotel. The club may be gone, but the drink remains—and happily so. It may be blushed in hue and frothy from the inclusion of egg white, but its herby, punchy snap of gin and fresh lemon juice gives it backbone and structure that are worth the lasting, decades-enduring adoration.

THE NOTES

Place 6 or 7 square ice cubes into a cocktail shaker. Pour in 2 fluid ounces (60ml) of gin, coating the ice. Add ½ fluid ounce (15ml) of fresh lemon juice, 2 teaspoons (10ml) of raspberry syrup, and 1 egg white. Shake in a vertical motion for 30 seconds. Strain slowly into a cocktail glass.

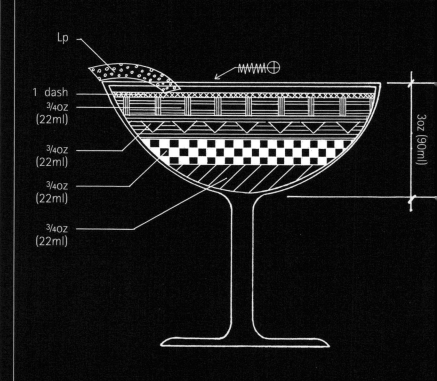

Lp

1 dash
3/4OZ (22ml)

3/4OZ (22ml)

3/4OZ (22ml)

3/4OZ (22ml)

3oz (90ml)

SPECIFICATIONS		EMBELLISHMENTS
////// Gin	▦▦▦ Cointreau	
▰ Lillet Blonde	✕✕✕✕ Absinthe	Lemon peel (Lp)
▽▽▽ Fresh lemon juice		

CORPSE REVIVER 2

Ever seen a beautiful old building wrapped in scaffolding only to reveal, months later, a sparkling-clean facade? Think of the Corpse Reviver 2 as that same scaffolding, only for you it's the morning-after tonic to a little too much evening indulgence. That is, in fact, the entire reason it was presumably created during the twist into the 20th century, making its print appearance in *The Savoy Cocktail Book* in 1930. Part quenching refresher, part smelling salt, the Corpse Reviver 2 (if you're wondering: yes, there is a Corpse Reviver 1, but, in my humble opinion, the second try was the charm) combines a bright burst of citrus with the herbal kick of gin and absinthe and the soothing quality of Cointreau. It also happens to be a nice alternative to the lovely but often-seen brunch-table staples—the Bloody Mary and the Bellini (see pages 22 and 16 for recipes).

THE NOTES

Place 6 or 7 square ice cubes into a cocktail shaker. Pour in ¾ fluid ounce (22ml) of gin, coating the ice. Add in ¾ fluid ounce (22ml) of Lillet Blonde, ¾ fluid ounce (22ml) of fresh lemon juice, ¾ fluid ounce (22ml) of Cointreau, and 1 dash of absinthe. Shake in a vertical motion for 30 seconds. Strain slowly into a coupe glass. Using a channel knife or standard vegetable peeler, gently slice only the skin (avoiding the bitter pith) of a lemon above the drink and drop the peel into the glass.

COSMOPOLITAN

It is undeniably true that the bartending cognoscenti of today follows the credo of What's Old Is Cool. But the Cosmo, as it's lovingly been nicknamed over the years (and, perhaps, fittingly, as its skyrocketing rise in popularity seems as far reaching as a constellation), shows no signs of becoming a quick flash-in-the-sky shooting star. You don't have to look far back to find its origins, but even so—as with much of cocktail lore—it's difficult to say who, exactly, invented it. What we do know is this: 1) Writer/bartender Toby Cecchini of New York City retooled the recipe to be the better version that it is today, kicking bottled, store-bought grenadine to the curb and using fresher ingredients in the mix; and 2) Were it not for the wildly popular television adaptation of Candace Bushnell's *Sex and the City*, Cosmo swilling may well have not seen the starry popularity it still appears to hold.

THE NOTES

Place 6 or 7 square ice cubes into a cocktail shaker. Pour in 1½ fluid ounces (45ml) of vodka, coating the ice. Add ½ fluid ounce (15ml) of Cointreau, 1 fluid ounce (30ml) of cranberry juice, and ¼ fluid ounce (8ml) of fresh lime juice. Shake in a vertical motion for 30 seconds. Strain slowly into a cocktail glass. Using a channel knife or standard vegetable peeler, gently slice only the skin (avoiding the bitter pith) of a lime above the drink and drop the peel into the glass.

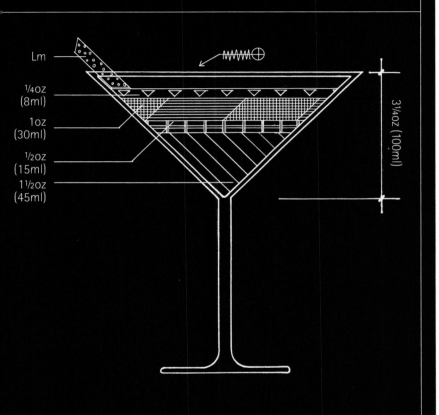

Lm

1/4oz
(8ml)

1oz
(30ml)

1/2oz
(15ml)

11/2oz
(45ml)

3¼oz (100ml)

SPECIFICATIONS

⬛ Vodka		⬛ Cranberry juice	
⬛ Cointreau		⬛ Fresh lime juice	

EMBELLISHMENTS

Lime peel
(Lm)

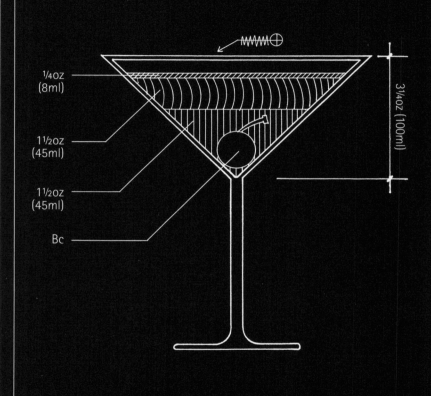

1/4OZ
(8ml)

1 1/2OZ
(45ml)

1 1/2OZ
(45ml)

Bc

3 1/4oz (100ml)

SPECIFICATIONS		EMBELLISHMENTS
Bourbon	Grenadine	
Madeira		Brandied cherry (Bc)

| 42 | CREOLE LADY |

CREOLE LADY

Fashion is a funny thing, be it in buildings or building drinks. But while the history of architecture nearly always provides a dependable connect-the-dots to the past, the history of cocktails is exactly the opposite: peering into the past more often than not provides a Magic 8 Ball answer of "Try again later!" The Creole Lady is a mysterious one—you can only take a cue from her name and ingredients as to who she is and where she came from. In all likelihood, she was a pre-Prohibition-era good-time gal, back in the day when both bourbon and Madeira reigned high on the list of popular sippers. Bourbon has certainly seen a righteous renaissance in the early 21st century; Madeira hasn't had the same success, but with the rising popularity and use of other fortified wines like port and sherry in cocktails, I suspect it's only a matter of time. Put this one on your playlist and you'll be ahead of the game.

THE NOTES

Drop a brandied cherry into a cocktail glass and then set aside. Place 6 or 7 square ice cubes into a cocktail shaker. Pour in 1½ fluid ounces (45ml) of bourbon coating the ice. Add in 1½ fluid ounces (45ml) of Madeira and ¼ fluid ounce (8ml) of grenadine. Shake in a vertical motion for 30 seconds. Strain slowly into the cocktail glass.

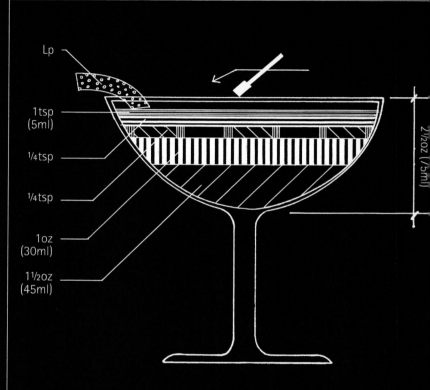

Lp

1tsp
(5ml)

¼tsp

¼tsp

1oz
(30ml)

1½oz
(45ml)

2½oz (75ml)

SPECIFICATIONS		EMBELLISHMENTS
///// Gin	▬▬▬ Green Chartreuse	
‖‖‖‖‖ Dry vermouth	▤▤▤ Fresh pineapple juice	Lemon peel (Lp)
▨▨ Kümmel		

CUBANO

A lot of things come to mind when you think of Cuba, and when it comes to cocktails, rum is certainly at the top of the list. But gin wasn't a complete stranger to this island nation, and some cocktail historians even claim that a tiny bit was added to the Cuba Libre—that famed rum-and-Coke concoction spritzed with lime juice. Maybe the thing to take away from such curious bits of information is this: drinks from or named for places with beaches and swaying palm trees should all but guarantee central air for the soul. The Cubano certainly falls easily into those borders. Bright, herby gin, Kümmel, vermouth, and Chartreuse get just a little whimsical kick in the madras shorts from a drizzle of sweet, refreshing pineapple juice. If you're searching for a sophisticated alternative to umbrella-clad tiki drinks, this is a great choice.

THE NOTES

Place 6 or 7 square ice cubes into a cocktail shaker. Pour in 1½ fluid ounces (45ml) of gin, coating the ice. Add in 1 fluid ounce (30ml) of dry vermouth, ¼ teaspoon of Kümmel, ¼ teaspoon of green Chartreuse, and 1 teaspoon (5ml) of fresh pineapple juice. Using a long bar spoon, quickly stir the cocktail's ingredients for 30 seconds. Strain slowly into a coupe glass. Using a channel knife or standard vegetable peeler, gently slice only the skin (avoiding the bitter pith) of a lemon above the drink and drop the peel into the glass.

DAIQUIRI

Three ingredients, that's it. Its simple construction speaks to the notion that to build something beautiful doesn't need to necessarily encompass inordinately complicated materials.

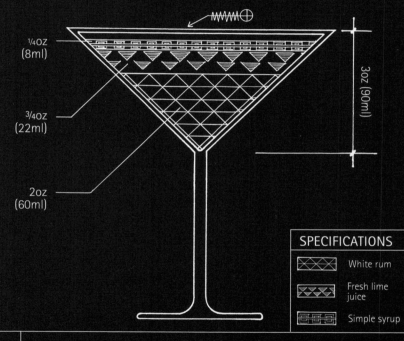

¼OZ (8ml)

¾OZ (22ml)

2oz (60ml)

3oz (90ml)

SPECIFICATIONS

White rum
Fresh lime juice
Simple syrup

THE NOTES

Place 6 or 7 square ice cubes into a cocktail shaker. Pour in 2 fluid ounces (60ml) of white rum, coating the ice. Add in ¾ fluid ounce (22ml) of fresh lime juice and ¼ fluid ounce (8ml) of simple syrup (see p. 53). Shake in a vertical motion for 30 seconds. Strain slowly into a cocktail glass.

DE RIGUEUR

Because honey is thick, it's better to make a honey syrup for cold drinks (two parts honey, one part water, simmered until the honey dissolves and is then allowed to cool).

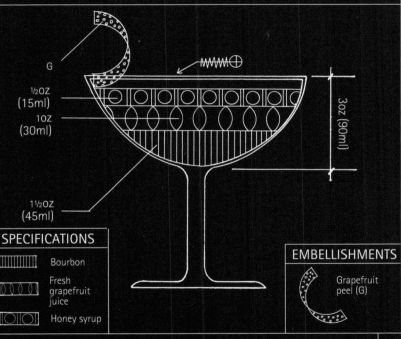

G

½OZ
(15ml)

1OZ
(30ml)

3oz (90ml)

1½OZ
(45ml)

SPECIFICATIONS

||||||||| Bourbon

〇〇〇〇 Fresh grapefruit juice

〇|〇| Honey syrup

EMBELLISHMENTS

Grapefruit peel (G)

THE NOTES

Place 6 or 7 square ice cubes into a cocktail shaker. Pour in 1½ fluid ounces (45ml) of bourbon, coating the ice. Add in 1 fluid ounce (30ml) of fresh grapefruit juice and ½ fluid ounce (15ml) of honey syrup. Shake in a vertical motion for 30 seconds. Strain slowly into a coupe glass. Using a channel knife or standard vegetable peeler, gently slice only the skin (avoiding the bitter pith) of a grapefruit above the drink and drop the peel into the glass.

EGGNOG

Like a wreath on a door, there's nothing else that signals the merriment of the holidays more than a bowl full of rich, nutmeg-spiced eggnog. True, well-crafted punches made a much welcome comeback in the 21st century, and this classic was ripe for a redo. After being mass-produced and relegated to milk containers on supermarket shelves, eggnog is well deserving of good ingredients and attention. Remember, when you're working with eggs (and this punch uses quite a few), keep them refrigerated until you are ready to use them and make sure your whisk-whipping arm is in tip-top shape.

THE NOTES

Crack 6 eggs into a large bowl (a punch bowl, if you have one) and, using a wire whisk, whip until frothy. Pour in ¾ cup (150g) of sugar and continue to whip until the color lightens. Next, thoroughly stir in 24 fluid ounces (700ml) of whole milk and 16 fluid ounces (480ml) of heavy cream. Add in 4 fluid ounces (120ml) each of bourbon and dark rum. Mix until well blended. Grate fresh nutmeg over the top and ladle into punch cups. Approx. 6 servings.

N

4oz
(120ml)

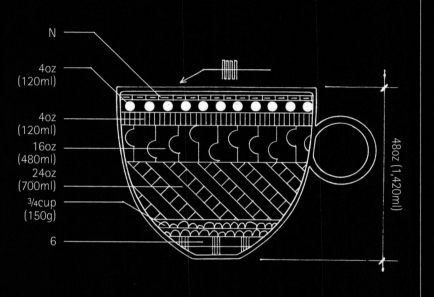

4oz
(120ml)

16oz
(480ml)

24oz
(700ml)

3/4 cup
(150g)

6

48oz (1,420ml)

SPECIFICATIONS

▦	Eggs (whole)	⟨⟨⟨⟨⟨⟨	Heavy cream
∿∿∿∿∿	Sugar	‖‖‖‖‖	Bourbon
▨	Whole milk	● ● ●	Dark rum

EMBELLISHMENTS

□□□□□□□□

Fresh grated n utmeg
(N)

EGGNOG   49

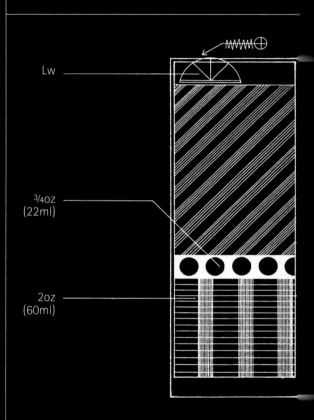

Lw

3/4oz
(22ml)

2oz
(60ml)

SPECIFICATIONS

Silver tequila		Ginger beer
Crème de cassis		

EL DIABLO

Tequila gets a bit of a bum rap among a portion of the agave-based spirit-drinking masses, relegated to shots tossed back quickly in a devil-may-care fashion or relegated solely to cocktails like the margarita. While the latter is certainly one of the world's most wonderful tipples (and appears among the 75 sippers in this book), there's a lot more versatility to tequila than it has been given credit for. One of the reasons I really love this drink is the addition of cassis, the currant-based liqueur that also tends to be sequestered to certain iconic drinks (the Kir Royale, in this case). But here, the earthy, slightly vegetal quality of tequila combines beautifully with the concentrated fruitiness of the cassis and the spice of ginger beer. It's familiar enough in flavor to be satisfying but with a great twist of ingredients that kick up both the spirit and liqueur into something entirely new. Make sure when buying tequila that the bottle states that it's 100% blue agave. Agave is the plant used to make tequila, so if it doesn't state that the spirit base is made entirely from it, it will be what is called *mixto*—about half agave, with the rest of the spirit gleaned from random sources of sugar. Read: headache!

THE NOTES

Place 6 or 7 square ice cubes into a cocktail shaker. Pour in 2 fluid ounces (60ml) of silver tequila, coating the ice. Add in ¾ fluid ounce (22ml) of crème de cassis. Shake in a vertical motion for 30 seconds. Strain slowly into an ice-filled Collins glass. Fill with ginger beer and garnish with a lime wedge.

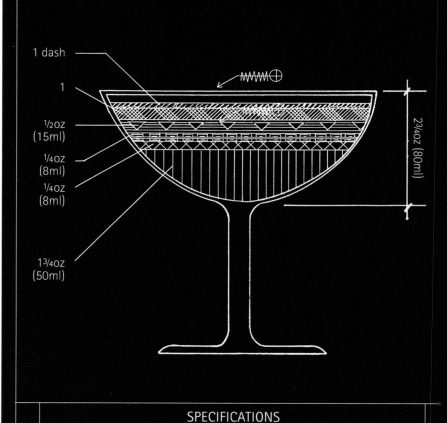

1 dash

1

½oz
(15ml)

¼oz
(8ml)

¼oz
(8ml)

1¾oz
(50ml)

2¾oz (80ml)

SPECIFICATIONS

Bourbon	Simple syrup	Egg white
Absinthe	Fresh lemon juice	Angostura bitters

FOX AND HOUNDS

I love this drink—as much for its hilarious lord-of-the-manor title as for its really interesting combination of ingredients. You've got bourbon's sweet and spicy influence, the herby punch of absinthe, the sweet-tart kick of fresh lemon juice, and every home bartender's easy balance tweaker, simple syrup (equal parts sugar and water, heated until the sugar dissolves and is then cooled), and the texturally inimitable egg white. If you don't have absinthe, Pernod will do as well. Hound-beckoning trumpet and trusty galloping steed not included.

THE NOTES

Place 6 or 7 square ice cubes into a cocktail shaker. Pour in 1¾ fluid ounces (50ml) of bourbon, coating the ice. Add in ¼ fluid ounce (8ml) of absinthe, ¼ fluid ounce (8ml) of simple syrup, and ½ fluid ounce (15ml) of fresh lemon juice. Drop in the egg white. Add in 1 dash of Angostura bitters. Shake vigorously in a vertical motion for 30 seconds. Strain slowly into a coupe glass.

FRENCH 75

It is kind of funny how a word can take on a life of its own, making a completely different impression than its initial intended use. Exhibit A: the French 75. This lovely brandy-based cocktail is an easy one to make and seems to be the epitome of winking cocktail sophistication, in part owing to its highfalutin ingredients (some go for the gusto with cognac and champagne; other sippers and shakers are more conservative with brandy and other forms of sparkling wine) and also that its name sounds like some kind of fab French disco. Au contraire! The French 75 was an automatic weapon used during World War I to keep enemies at bay.

THE NOTES

Place 6 or 7 square ice cubes into a cocktail shaker. Pour in 1½ fluid ounces (45ml) of brandy, coating the ice. Add in ½ fluid ounce (15ml) of fresh lemon juice and ½ fluid ounce (15ml) of simple syrup (see p. 53). Shake in a vertical motion for 30 seconds. Strain slowly into a wineglass and top with 1 fluid ounce (30ml) of dry sparkling wine.

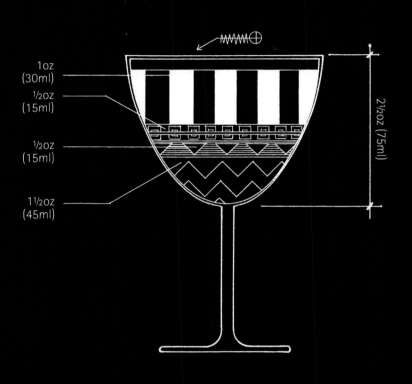

1oz
(30ml)

1/2oz
(15ml)

1/2oz
(15ml)

1 1/2oz
(45ml)

2 1/2oz (75ml)

SPECIFICATIONS

◁▷	Brandy	▦▦▦	Simple syrup
▨▨▨	Fresh lemon juice	▮▮▮	Sparkling wine

GIN RICKEY

The ultimate summerade to sip when the grill is on and the heat is spiking into Hadeslike proportions. Rickeys are super simple—citrus, spirit, soda. That's it.

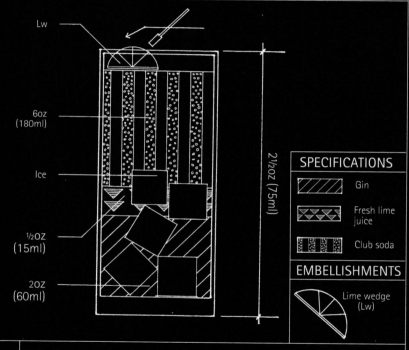

SPECIFICATIONS

/////	Gin
▽▽▽▽	Fresh lime juice
▦▦▦	Club soda

EMBELLISHMENTS

Lime wedge (Lw)

Lw

6oz (180ml)

Ice

½OZ (15ml)

2OZ (60ml)

2½oz (75ml)

THE NOTES

Place 5 or 6 square ice cubes into a highball glass. Pour in 2 fluid ounces (60ml) of gin, coating the ice. Add in ½ fluid ounce (15ml) of fresh lime juice. Using a long bar spoon, quickly stir the cocktail's ingredients for 30 seconds. Top with 6 fluid ounces (180ml) of club soda and garnish with a lime wedge.

HANKY-PANKY

This cocktail was created by Ada Coleman, the head bartender at the American Bar at the Savoy in London, around the turn of the last century for actor Charles Hawtrey. This play on sweet and bitter flavors made the thespian exclaim, "By Jove! That is the real hanky-panky!" when he sampled it. And so a drink was born.

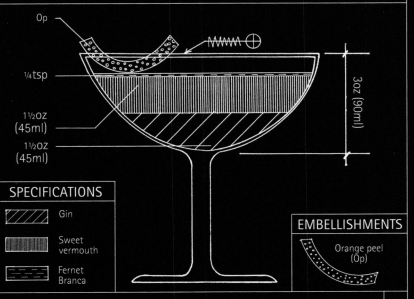

Op

¼tsp

1½OZ
(45ml)

1½OZ
(45ml)

3oz (90ml)

SPECIFICATIONS

Gin

Sweet
vermouth

Fernet
Branca

EMBELLISHMENTS

Orange peel
(Op)

THE NOTES

Place 6 or 7 square ice cubes into a cocktail shaker. Pour in 1½ fluid ounces (45ml) of gin, coating the ice. Add in 1½ fluid ounces (45ml) of sweet vermouth and ¼ teaspoon of Fernet Branca. Shake in a vertical motion for 30 seconds. Strain slowly into a coupe glass. Using a channel knife or standard vegetable peeler, gently slice only the skin (avoiding the bitter pith) of an orange above the drink and drop the peel into the glass.

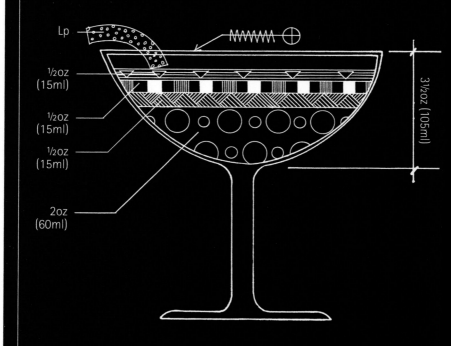

Lp

1/2oz
(15ml)

1/2oz
(15ml)

1/2oz
(15ml)

2oz
(60ml)

3½oz (105ml)

SPECIFICATIONS			EMBELLISHMENTS
Apple brandy		Orange curaçao	Lemon peel (Lp)
Bénédictine		Fresh lemon juice	

HONEYMOON

The name of this cocktail is entirely apt considering it was invented during Hollywood's Golden Age—the sort of honeymoon period for film, when being a celebrity meant you were famous for being an actor and not, say, flashing your undergarments or being the step-child of a once-famous athlete. A product of the Brown Derby—that chain of LA-centric eateries whose Hollywood outpost was the celluloid-centric spot to see and be seen—the Honeymoon is ready for a remake—or, at least, a revisit. As is its main ingredient, apple brandy. While you can certainly go for a French calvados, I like using applejack (i.e., American apple brandy) from Laird's in Scobeyville, New Jersey—the oldest (and, for quite some time, only) apple brandy producer in the U.S., which has been owned by the same family since its inception more than 300 years ago.

THE NOTES

Place 6 or 7 square ice cubes into a cocktail shaker. Pour in 2 fluid ounces (60ml) of apple brandy, coating the ice. Add in ½ fluid ounce (15ml) of Bénédictine, ½ fluid ounce (15ml) of orange curaçao, and ½ fluid ounce (15ml) of fresh lemon juice. Shake in a vertical motion for 30 seconds. Strain slowly into a coupe glass. Using a channel knife or standard vegetable peeler, gently slice only the skin (avoiding the bitter pith) of a lemon above the drink and drop the peel into the glass.

HURRICANE

This was the very first drink I had on my very first visit to New Orleans, LA, at the famed watering hole Pat O'Brien's. We sat in the middle of the courtyard in the glow of their iconic flaming water fountain, sipping and smiling at such a great introduction to the Crescent City, but . . . the drink honestly wasn't that great. Or, it tasted like it could have been great, or great at one time, but it was saccharine-sweet and tasted just a little bit artificial. But it certainly doesn't have to be that way. The drink was apparently named for the popular hurricane-lamp style of streetlight enclosures, so lovely along NOLA's wrought-iron-balcony-lined throughways in the French Quarter, but unfortunately, the circa-1930s spot sells (and possibly serves) a fast and easy premixed version of the drink these days to keep up with the high demand of Big Easy celebrants waiting in line to get in. Instead of succumbing to the just-add-liquor notion, try this tropical, heady mixer via fresh, good ingredients—it's more than worth the effort. And it may be one of the only grown-up opportunities for you to drink through a bendy straw without irony.

THE NOTES

Place 6 or 7 square ice cubes into a cocktail shaker. Pour in 2 fluid ounces (60ml) of dark rum and 2 fluid ounces (60ml) of light rum, coating the ice. Add in 1 fluid ounce (30ml) of fresh orange juice, 1 fluid ounce (30ml) of fresh passion fruit juice, ½ fluid ounce (15ml) of fresh lime juice, and ¼ teaspoon of simple syrup (see p. 53). Shake in a vertical motion for 30 seconds. Strain slowly into an ice-filled hurricane glass. Garnish with an orange wheel.

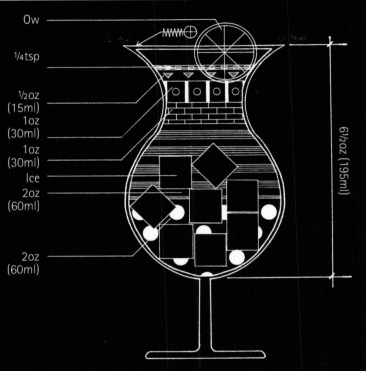

Ow

¼tsp

½oz
(15ml)
1oz
(30ml)

1oz
(30ml)

Ice

2oz
(60ml)

2oz
(60ml)

6½oz (195ml)

SPECIFICATIONS

- ●●● Dark rum
- Light rum
- Fresh orange juice
- ○○○ Fresh passion fruit juice
- ▽▽▽ Fresh lime juice
- Simple syrup

EMBELLISHMENTS

Orange wheel (Ow)

JACK ROSE

Make your own grenadine. Stir together two parts pomegranate juice and one part sugar and bring them to a boil. Turn down the heat and allow to simmer for between 20 and 30 minutes. Allow to cool, add in a few dashes of orange flower water, and keep for up to a month in a sealed container in your refrigerator.

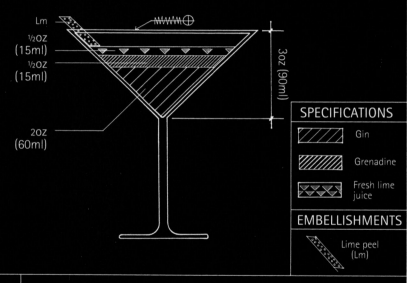

Lm

½OZ
(15ml)

½OZ
(15ml)

2OZ
(60ml)

3oz (90ml)

SPECIFICATIONS

Gin

Grenadine

Fresh lime juice

EMBELLISHMENTS

Lime peel
(Lm)

THE NOTES

Place 6 or 7 square ice cubes into a cocktail shaker. Pour in 2 fluid ounces (60ml) of gin, coating the ice. Add in ½ fluid ounce (15ml) of grenadine and ½ fluid ounce (15ml) of fresh lime juice. Shake in a vertical motion for 30 seconds. Strain slowly into a cocktail glass. Using a channel knife or standard vegetable peeler, gently slice only the skin (avoiding the bitter pith) of a lime above the drink and drop the peel into the glass.

KIR ROYALE

Although it's often relegated to the brunch table, the Kir Royale—with its pretty plum hue and towerlike appearance in a long, slender champagne flute—makes a great aperitif, too. One of its key ingredients, crème de cassis, is made from blackcurrants and is said to have been invented in Burgundy, France.

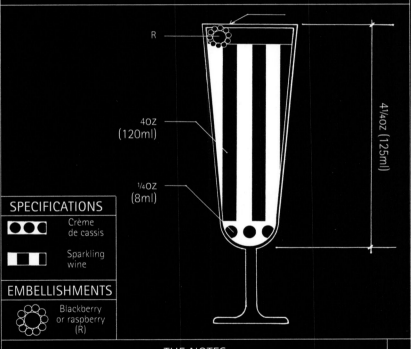

R

4OZ
(120ml)

¼OZ
(8ml)

4¼OZ (125ml)

SPECIFICATIONS

Crème
de cassis

Sparkling
wine

EMBELLISHMENTS

Blackberry
or raspberry
(R)

THE NOTES

Pour ¼ fluid ounce (8ml) of crème de cassis into a champagne flute. Top with 4 fluid ounces (120ml) of dry sparkling wine. Garnish with a fresh blackberry or raspberry.

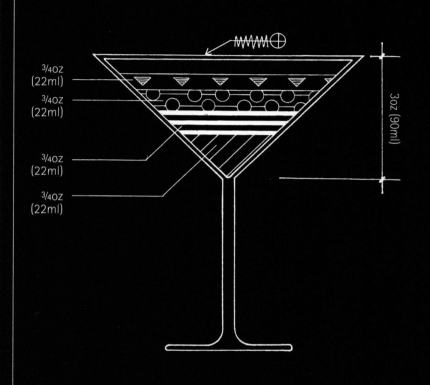

¾OZ
(22ml)

¾OZ
(22ml)

¾OZ
(22ml)

¾OZ
(22ml)

3oz (90ml)

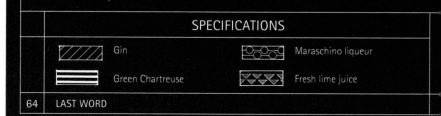

SPECIFICATIONS

	Gin		Maraschino liqueur
	Green Chartreuse		Fresh lime juice

LAST WORD

You know the old-school, white-glove ritual of bestowing a demure dish of sorbet between courses as a chilly, palate-cleansing treat to pleasantly ready you for the next course? If it were up to me, I'd sub in the Last Word for that frozen treat instead. Herbaceous and tongue-whippingly bright, the Last Word's history is hard to pinpoint, but judging by its ingredients, in all likelihood it dates to the clever cocktail-crafting era of pre-Prohibition. Chartreuse, gin, maraschino liqueur, fresh lime juice—the three come together to make the most wonderful of sweet-tart concoctions, perfect as a refresher for a warm, sunny day in the backyard—or a delicious palate cleanser between courses at your next dinner party. Note that the drink is best with equal parts of all ingredients, so feel free to go up or down to make more or less.

THE NOTES

Place 6 or 7 square ice cubes into a cocktail shaker. Pour in ¾ fluid ounce (22ml) of gin, coating the ice. Add in ¾ fluid ounce (22ml) of green Chartreuse, ¾ fluid ounce (22ml) of maraschino liqueur, and ¾ fluid ounce (22ml) of fresh lime juice. Shake in a vertical motion for 30 seconds. Strain slowly into a cocktail glass.

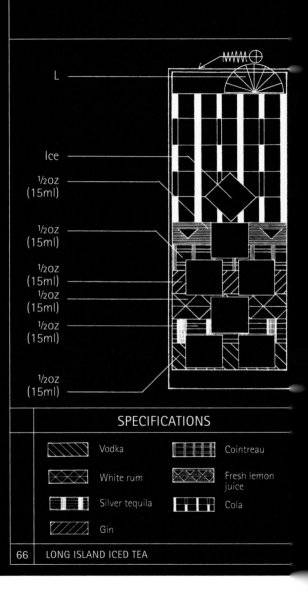

L

Ice

½oz
(15ml)

½oz
(15ml)

½oz
(15ml)

½oz
(15ml)

½oz
(15ml)

½oz
(15ml)

SPECIFICATIONS

Vodka		Cointreau	
White rum		Fresh lemon juice	
Silver tequila		Cola	
Gin			

LONG ISLAND ICED TEA

The whole point of this drink back in the 80s was about... How do I put this lightly? About the fast effects of its ingredients. And surely, the ton of falling bricks that too many Long Island Iced Teas can create is enough to rattle anyone's foundation. But it's also a clever combination that makes for a refreshing and deceptively easy-drinking delight. As with the Last Word (see pages 64–65), note that the measurements are equal, so if you want to dial it down, cut the spirit measurements in half and just use a little more cola.

THE NOTES

Place 6 or 7 square ice cubes into a cocktail shaker. Pour in ½ fluid ounce (15ml) of vodka, coating the ice. Add in ½ fluid ounce (15ml) of silver tequila, ½ fluid ounce (15ml) of white rum, ½ fluid ounce (15ml) of gin, ½ fluid ounce (15ml) of Cointreau, and ½ fluid ounce (15ml) of fresh lemon juice. Shake in a vertical motion for 30 seconds. Strain slowly into an ice-filled Collins glass. Top with cola. Using a long bar spoon, stir briefly to blend. Garnish with a lemon wedge.

MAI TAI

Legendary barman Victor Bergeron created this fruity, heady concoction at his famed California cocktail stable, Trader Vic's. It might just seem like a fruity fandango of any ol' spirit and juice, but the secret to nailing it all together perfectly is the just-right mix of sweet and sour, as well as a special little foundational flourish of orgeat, a sweet, cloudy almond-flavored syrup. Make sure to add that (which also happens to be delicious mixed with seltzer water for a refreshing, alcohol-free sipper) and you'll have built a legend, too.

THE NOTES

Place 6 or 7 square ice cubes into a cocktail shaker. Pour in 2 fluid ounces (60ml) of dark rum, coating the ice. Add in ¾ fluid ounce (22ml) of orange curaçao, ¾ fluid ounce (22ml) of fresh lime juice, and ½ fluid ounce (15ml) of orgeat syrup. Shake in a vertical motion for 30 seconds. Strain slowly into an ice-filled rocks glass. Using a channel knife or standard vegetable peeler, gently slice only the skin (avoiding the bitter pith) of a lime above the drink and drop the peel into the glass.

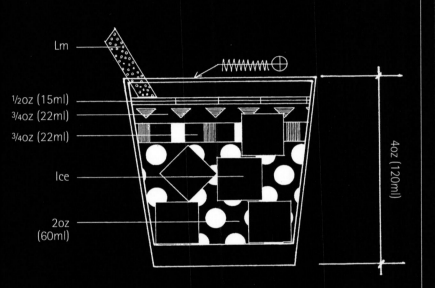

Lm

1/2oz (15ml)
3/4oz (22ml)

3/4oz (22ml)

Ice

2oz
(60ml)

4oz (120ml)

SPECIFICATIONS

- Dark rum
- Orange curaçao
- Fresh lime juice
- Orgeat syrup

EMBELLISHMENTS

Lime peel (Lm)

MANHATTAN

Can you think of a new-world city more architecturally breathtaking? That skyline! Those lights! I've lived in New York City for more than two decades, and the sight of it still makes me sigh when I approach the city and see that borough's skyscape on the horizon. To have a drink named after it must mean it's pretty special. The Manhattan—whiskey (rye or bourbon), sweet vermouth, Angostura bitters, a cherry on top—is my favorite drink name after my favorite borough of my favorite city. Bias? Yes! But for a whiskey lover, it's genius—the vermouth softens the edges of the whiskey complementing the notes it picks up from barrel aging; the bitters pluck the strings of the savory side of this cocktail; and the cherry? Well, hell. That's just fun.

THE NOTES

Place 6 or 7 square ice cubes into a cocktail shaker. Pour in 2 fluid ounces (60ml) of rye (or bourbon if you prefer), coating the ice. Add in 1 fluid ounce (30ml) of sweet vermouth and 3 dashes of Angostura bitters. Using a long bar spoon, stir the cocktail's ingredients for 30 seconds. Strain slowly into a cocktail glass. Garnish with a brandied cherry.

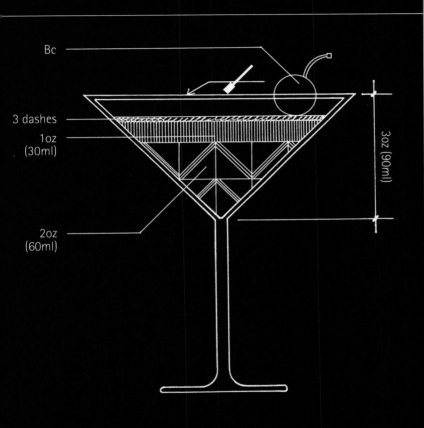

Bc

3 dashes

1oz
(30ml)

2oz
(60ml)

3oz (90ml)

SPECIFICATIONS		EMBELLISHMENTS	
Rye or bourbon	Angostura bitters	Brandied cherry (Bc)	
Sweet vermouth			

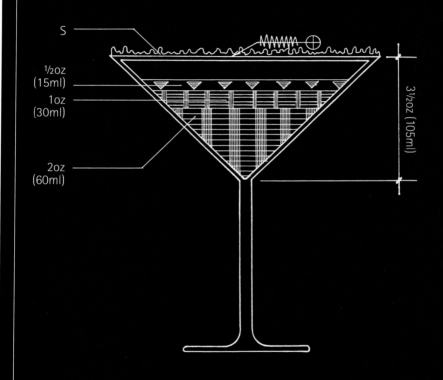

S

½oz
(15ml)

1oz
(30ml)

2oz
(60ml)

3½oz (105ml)

SPECIFICATIONS		EMBELLISHMENTS
Silver tequila	Fresh lime juice	
Cointreau		*Sel gris*, or other coarse salt (S)

MARGARITA

Oh, the lovely Margarita. This gorgeous mix of fresh citrus, good tequila (always, always buy a bottle that says "100% blue agave"—anything else will be something called *mixto*, which is little more than half blue agave and the rest an odd-lot additive mix of sugar sources; read: headache), and orange liqueur (Cointreau is a good-quality bet) is perfect in its balanced simplicity. Yet there are a gazillion ways to take its unbeatable structure and turn it into a sticky-sweet collapsible house of cards. So repeat after me: simple is good! Which isn't to discourage you from other versions—say, muddling up some fresh strawberries or adding in some fresh peach purée to add an extra dimension to the drink—but when it comes to the basics, never shortcut with store-bought mixes or crazy blender tricks and you will be deliciously rewarded every time.

THE NOTES

Using the discarded lime from the juicing required for this cocktail, run the squeezed flesh around the rim of a cocktail glass. Sprinkle *sel gris* into a dish and dip the rim of the glass in the salt. Set aside. Place 6 or 7 square ice cubes into a cocktail shaker. Pour in 2 fluid ounces (60ml) of silver tequila, coating the ice. Add in 1 fluid ounce (30ml) of Cointreau and ½ fluid ounce (15ml) fresh lime juice. Shake in a vertical motion for 30 seconds. Strain slowly into the cocktail glass.

1tsp
(5ml)

2½oz
(75ml)

0

2½oz (75ml)

SPECIFICATIONS		EMBELLISHMENTS
Gin	Dry vermouth	Green olive (0)

74 MARTINI

MARTINI

There has been more written about the Martini—the pinnacle, Big Daddy, end all, be all of all drinks—than, possibly, the topics of *War and Peace*. An exaggeration? I think not. Its potential origins (the Martinez, among other claims to fame), the best way to make one, the presence or absence of vermouth, to adhere solely to Team Gin or deflect to Team Vodka. But, the thing is, a Martini is maybe a little more like modular furniture than concrete footings more adaptable to personal taste than trapped in scaffolding. With that said, I'm a fan of gin and vermouth. I also adore olives of all kinds, although a good, firm-fleshed green sort (hold the pimiento) is a better match for the herby flavors of the other ingredients. With that said, this is my general setup for a Martini, but feel free to move things around as you like. There is one thing I will try to impress upon you, though. Don't shake it. The ice bruises the clear spirit, making it foggy instead of the crystal clear vision I believe this drink ought to be.

THE NOTES

Place 6 or 7 square ice cubes into a cocktail shaker. Pour in 2½ fluid ounces (75ml) of gin, coating the ice. Add in 1 teaspoon (5ml) of dry vermouth. Using a long bar spoon, stir the cocktail's ingredients for 30 seconds. Place one olive in a cocktail glass and strain slowly into it.

MINT JULEP

The wonderful southern American style of the Mint Julep is a genius bit of local sourcing for the Bluegrass State: Kentucky-made bourbon (no, it doesn't have to come from Kentucky to be deemed bourbon—that, dear thirsty friends, is a myth); mint plucked from the garden; a bit of sugar from the kitchen; crushed ice from the freezer. When the weather turns warm, it's the kind of lazy-day cocktail that you don't have to wander too far afield to make (and thank goodness).

THE NOTES

Drop 3 or 4 good-sized fresh mint leaves into the bottom of a highball glass. Pour in ½ fluid ounce (15ml) of simple syrup (see p. 53) and gently press into the mint and liquid with a muddler. Add about 1 cup of crushed ice. Pour in 2 fluid ounces (60ml) of bourbon. Using a long bar spoon, stir the cocktail's ingredients for 30 seconds. Garnish with a mint sprig.

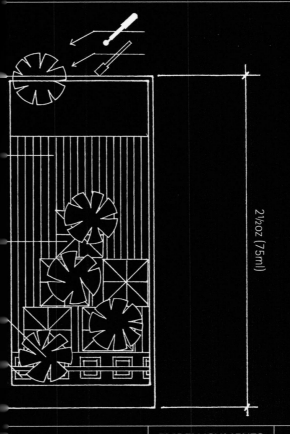

2½oz (75ml)

SPECIFICATIONS		EMBELLISHMENTS	
⬛ Bourbon		Mint sprig (Ms)	

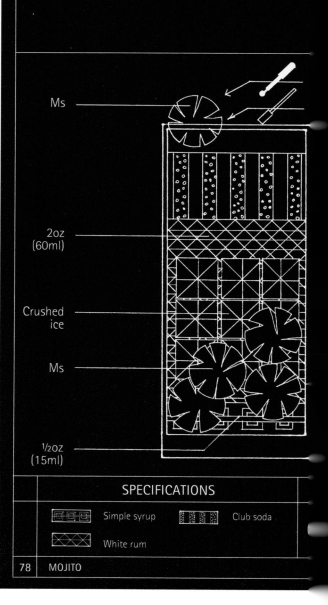

Ms

2oz
(60ml)

Crushed
ice

Ms

1/2oz
(15ml)

SPECIFICATIONS

	Simple syrup			Club soda
	White rum			

MOJITO

It's fitting that this drink comes on the tail of the Mint Julep, as the building of each is incredibly similar and based on the same principles of gently bruising mint leaves with sugar syrup to release their aromatic and flavorful oils, not to mention the easy-ingredient mix of materials that doesn't require that you reach for a shaker and strainer. But, instead of the American South, the Mojito hails from balmy, beautiful Cuba—which means substituting bourbon for rum.

THE NOTES

Drop 3 or 4 good-sized fresh mint leaves into the bottom of a highball glass. Pour in ½ fluid ounce (15ml) of simple syrup and gently press into the mint and liquid with a muddler. Add about 1 cup of crushed ice. Pour in 2 fluid ounces (60ml) of white rum. Using a long bar spoon, stir the cocktail's ingredients for 30 seconds. Top with club soda and garnish with a mint sprig.

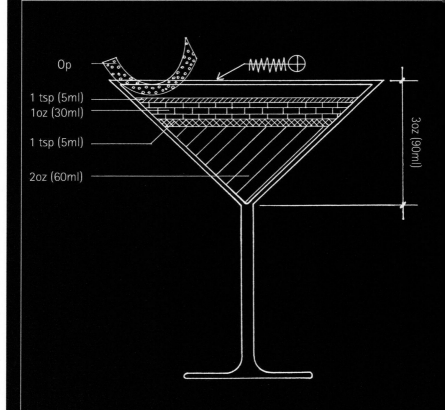

Op

1 tsp (5ml)
1oz (30ml)

1 tsp (5ml)

2oz (60ml)

3oz (90ml)

	SPECIFICATIONS		EMBELLISHMENTS
	///// Gin	▦ Fresh orange juice	Orange peel (Op)
	▧ Absinthe	///// Grenadine	
80	MONKEY GLAND		

MONKEY GLAND

The story goes that the odd name of this cocktail is a nod to the (how shall I put it?) creative surgical techniques of one Dr. Serge Voronoff, who believed that gland transplants were more effective for curing certain ailments attached to human glandular malfunction then attempting to correct, say, a thyroid problem via an injectable medicine. Needless to say, the attachment of animal glands to that of a human's fell out of favor, but what might have fallen into dusty, oddball medical history lives on in this curious tipple—whose combination of ingredients is far more appetizing than Dr. Voronoff's techniques.

THE NOTES

Place 6 or 7 square ice cubes into a cocktail shaker. Pour in 2 fluid ounces (60ml) of gin, coating the ice. Add in 1 teaspoon (5ml) of absinthe, 1 fluid ounce (30ml) of fresh orange juice, and 1 teaspoon (5ml) of grenadine. Shake in a vertical motion for 30 seconds. Strain slowly into a cocktail glass. Using a channel knife or standard vegetable peeler, gently slice only the skin (avoiding the bitter pith) of an orange above the drink and drop the peel into the glass.

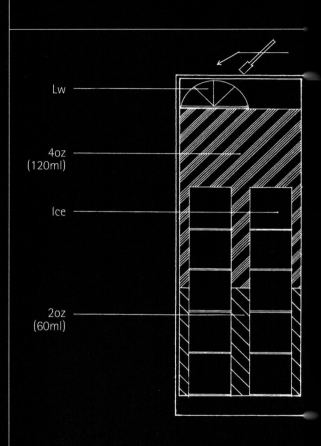

Lw

4oz
(120ml)

Ice

2oz
(60ml)

SPECIFICATIONS

| | Vodka | | Ginger beer |

MOSCOW MULE

Improvement in materials—and the good distribution of them—has utterly changed the way certain drinks taste in modern-day cocktail culture. Exhibit A: the Moscow Mule. This drink is unmemorable with your average, everyday sugary versions of ginger ale that have long been readily available on the market. But with ginger beer? Mmmm. This vodka-based refresher becomes something spicy, eye-opening, and with a kick (like from a mule, get it?) that comes from both the spirit and gingery influence.

THE NOTES

Fill a Collins glass with ice. Pour in 2 fluid ounces (60ml) of vodka, coating the ice. Add in 4 fluid ounces (120ml) of ginger beer. Stir briefly with a long bar spoon. Garnish with a lime wedge.

OLD-FASHIONED

The funny thing about this drink is that it implies a firm, sentimental kind of stability to its base. Well, as things sometimes turn out, the Old-Fashioned has a little bit of a Hatfield and McCoy warring faction on the use, or lack thereof, of proper materials here. Some prefer this drink with a muddled orange slice and cherry. Others do not. I fall into the latter category, if only because I find the addition of those extra materials to be cumbersome, and I prefer the sleek design of the fruitless and muddleless here. Experiment as you will, but in an Old-Fashioned, less, I believe, is more.

THE NOTES

Drop 1 sugar cube into a rocks glass. Drip 2 or 3 dashes of Angostura bitters onto it. Using a muddler or wooden spoon, crush the cube. Add in 4 or 5 ice cubes and pour 2 fluid ounces (60ml) of rye over the ice. Stir for about 10 seconds. Using a channel knife or standard vegetable peeler, gently slice only the skin (avoiding the bitter pith) of an orange above the drink and drop the peel into the glass.

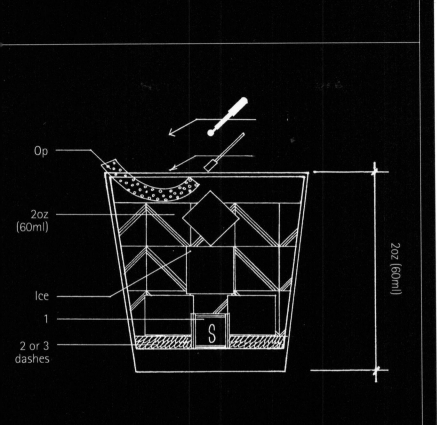

Op

2oz
(60ml)

Ice

1

2 or 3
dashes

2oz (60ml)

SPECIFICATIONS		EMBELLISHMENTS	
S Sugar cube	Rye	Orange peel (Op)	
Angostura bitters			

PARISIAN BLONDE

French women don't get fat, or so we are told. How this could be at all possible eating all that great cheese, foie gras, and fresh daily bread seems a feat of impossibility, but perhaps, like the unmatched magic of Paris itself, there are some mysteries that shall remain just that. So after washing down her wonderful baguette smeared in rich foie gras with a glass of Sauternes, eating chèvre by the spoonful, and finishing off with a rich, custardy mille-feuille, perhaps the heroine of our story can end her meal with one of these. Vive la France!

THE NOTES

Place 6 or 7 square ice cubes into a cocktail shaker. Pour in 1 fluid ounce (30ml) of dark rum, coating the ice. Add in 1 fluid ounce (30ml) of orange curaçao and 1 fluid ounce (30ml) of cream. Shake in a vertical motion for 30 seconds. Strain slowly into a coupe glass. Garnish with fresh grated cinnamon.

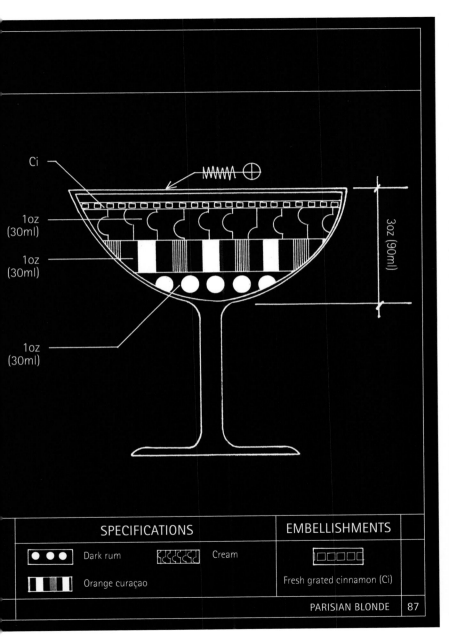

Ci

1oz
(30ml)

1oz
(30ml)

1oz
(30ml)

3oz (90ml)

SPECIFICATIONS		EMBELLISHMENTS	
● ● ● Dark rum	Cream		
Orange curaçao		Fresh grated cinnamon (Ci)	
		PARISIAN BLONDE	87

PENDENNIS

Sometimes opposites attract—metal and wood, glass and concrete—materials that seem at odds in some ways but together create a physical and visual kind of texture that's pleasing to the beholder. Cocktails can be like this, too—the Pendennis being an excellent example of individual things that seem at odds but somehow create a final product that is more than the sum of its parts. Here the idea of gin, apricot brandy, bitters, citrus, and simple syrup might seem somehow like a mix that doesn't quite meld, but it does. The Pendennis is complex without being puzzling, delicious without being one-note.

THE NOTES

Place 6 or 7 square ice cubes into a cocktail shaker. Pour in 2 fluid ounces (60ml) of gin, coating the ice. Add in 1 fluid ounce (30ml) of apricot brandy, ½ fluid ounce (15ml) of fresh lime juice, 1 teaspoon (5ml) of simple syrup (see p.53), and 2 dashes of Peychaud's Bitters. Shake in a vertical motion for 30 seconds. Strain slowly into a cocktail glass.

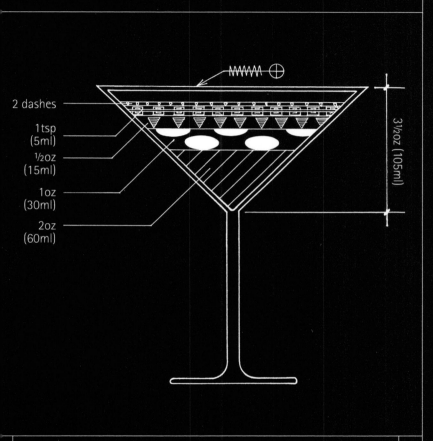

2 dashes

1tsp
(5ml)

1/2oz
(15ml)

1oz
(30ml)

2oz
(60ml)

3 1/2oz (105ml)

SPECIFICATIONS

/////	Gin	◄◄◄◄	Fresh lime juice	◊◊◊◊◊	Peychaud's Bitters	
◖●●◗	Apricot brandy	▭▭▭	Simple syrup			

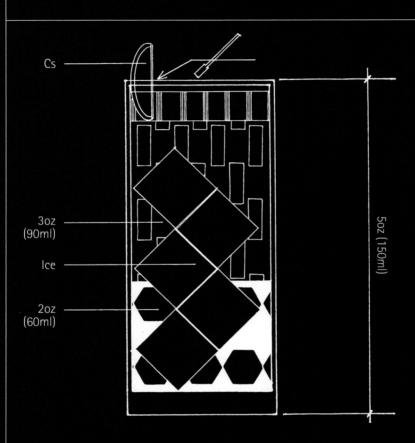

Cs

3oz
(90ml)

Ice

2oz
(60ml)

5oz (150ml)

SPECIFICATIONS		EMBELLISHMENTS
Pimm's No. 1	Lemonade	
Lemon-lime soda		Cucumber stick (Cs)

PIMM'S CUP

I really can't think of a better thing to sip—other than, perhaps, lemonade—on the hottest of hot summer days. But Pimm's actually began as an accompaniment to oyster slurping in England in the 19th century, when bar owner James Pimm doctored up the local rough-tasting gin with fruit extracts and liqueurs—and that went down well, indeed. The Pimm's Cup—low in alcohol and yet dizzyingly easy to drink quite a few of—mixes Pimm's gin-based No. 1 (there are other versions on the market, based with everything from brandy to vodka) with lemon-lime soda, a splash of lemonade, and the all-important cucumber stick.

THE NOTES

Place 5 or 6 square ice cubes into a highball glass. Pour in 2 fluid ounces (60ml) of Pimm's No. 1, allowing the two to mingle with the ice for a moment. Pour in 3 fluid ounces (90ml) of lemon-lime soda and top with lemonade. Using a long bar spoon, stir for about 10 seconds. Garnish with a cucumber stick.

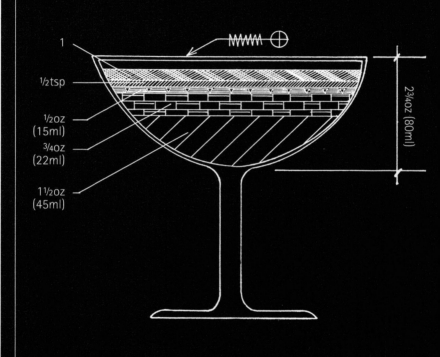

1

½tsp

½oz
(15ml)

¾oz
(22ml)

1½oz
(45ml)

2¾oz (80ml)

SPECIFICATIONS

	Gin		Fresh lemon juice		Egg white
	Applejack		Grenadine		

92 PINK LADY

PINK LADY

I like to think of the Pink Lady as the slightly more sophisticated cousin of the Parisian Blonde (she is a lady, after all). The name comes from the addition of grenadine, which adds a pinkish hue to the final color of the drink, but that is one of the only materials that has remained consistent in this cocktail over the years, which became more and more simplified (egg white traded for cream; applejack left out entirely; lemon thrown to the wayside). It's worth it, though, to make this in its presumably original form (again—cocktail history is a slippery slope; one man's truth is another man's folly).

THE NOTES

Place 6 or 7 square ice cubes into a cocktail shaker. Pour in 1½ fluid ounces (45ml) of gin, coating the ice. Add in ¾ fluid ounce (22ml) of applejack, ½ fluid ounce (15ml) of fresh lemon juice, ½ teaspoon (5ml) of grenadine, and 1 egg white. Shake in a vertical motion for 30 seconds. Strain slowly into a cocktail glass.

PISCO SOUR

Is it Peruvian? Is it Chilean? The debate has raged for centuries, and no one's giving in anytime soon. Pisco—a brandylike spirit that may well have its origins with the Spanish explorers who roamed the Americas in the 16th century, bringing grape-growing knowledge and, presumably, the science of distillation. Regardless of who wins the battle of origin, the Pisco Sour—a refreshing concoction of its namesake spirit, lime, simple syrup or sugar, egg white, and bitters—is the national sipper to toss back in both countries. One thing does appear certain, though, in the murky history that is cocktails: the architect of the drink was Utah native Victor Vaughn Morris, who moved to Peru in the early 20th century and opened a bar in Lima.

THE NOTES

Place 6 or 7 square ice cubes into a cocktail shaker. Pour in 1½ fluid ounces (45ml) of pisco, coating the ice. Add in ½ fluid ounce (15ml) of fresh lime juice, ¾ fluid ounce (22ml) of simple syrup, and 1 egg white. Shake in a vertical motion for 30 seconds. Strain slowly into a coupe glass. Drip 3 dashes of Angostura bitters over the top.

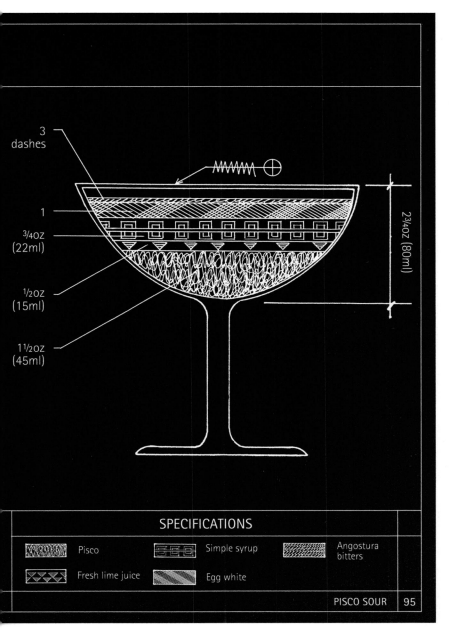

3
dashes

1

3/4oz
(22ml)

1/2oz
(15ml)

1 1/2oz
(45ml)

2 3/4oz (80ml)

SPECIFICATIONS

▨ Pisco	🔲 Simple syrup	▨ Angostura bitters
▽ Fresh lime juice	▨ Egg white		

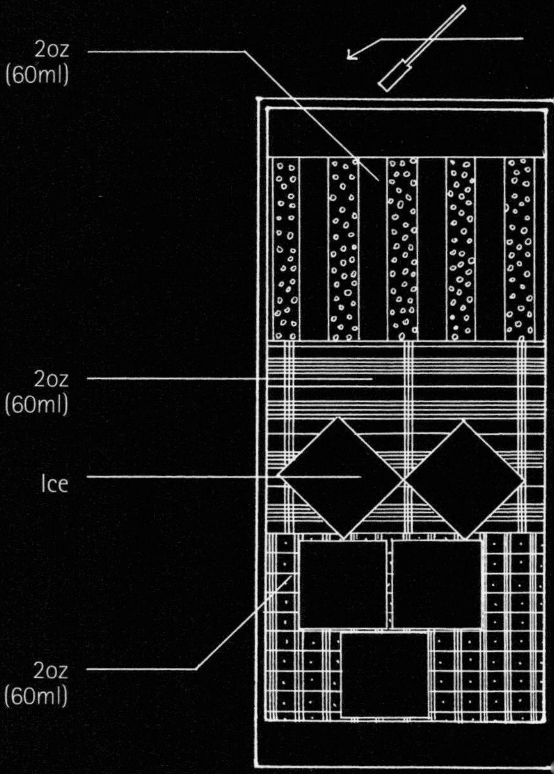
2oz
(60ml)
2oz
(60ml)
Ice
2oz
(60ml)

SPECIFICATIONS

Blended Scotch whiskey

Ginger ale

PRESBYTERIAN

I had the good fortune to sip my very first Presbyterian in what I consider its homeland: Scotland. I've seen this drink made with all sorts of whiskies—American, Irish (blasphemy!), Canadian—but if we're going to have to go on instinct minus any actual inked proof of the drink's rooted past, my guess is to go with the most obvious. In this case, the Church of Scotland and the drink's primary and best ingredient: good blended Scotch whiskey (and, no, you can't deem a spirit Scotch unless it comes from Scotland—just try; they have a team of lawyers at the ready who will come after you). But let's not get a bee in our wee bonny bonnets—this is a simple drink and a deliciously simple pleasure to sip.

THE NOTES

Place 5 or 6 square ice cubes into a highball glass. Pour in 2 fluid ounces (60ml) of blended Scotch whiskey, coating the ice. Add in 2 fluid ounces (60ml) each of good-quality ginger ale and club soda and stir briefly with a bar spoon.

PRESIDENTE

Being president of anything, let alone a country, is a hard job. Of course, one should expect to have a drink specifically created for the auspicious position (because, truly, with such trying tasks at hand, one needs a bit of refreshment every now and again). Popular lore has it that the president in question was Fulgencio Batista's predecessor in Cuba—General Carmen Menocal; however, there were nearly a dozen presidents and provisional presidents in the time between Menocal's rule and Batista's—and Menocal's first name was actually Mario, not Carmen. Still, Mario García Menocal ruled the tiny island nation from 1913 to 1921, and as the Presidente was created in the 1920s and Menocal was a big part of fighting to gain Cuba's independence from Spain, I'm happy to hand him the prize. However you craft your spirited history, though, it's a lovely, sophisticated rum-based drink.

THE NOTES

Place 6 or 7 square ice cubes into a cocktail shaker. Pour in 1¾ fluid ounces (50ml) of white rum, coating the ice. Add in ½ fluid ounce (15ml) of dry vermouth, ½ fluid ounce (15ml) of orange curaçao, and ¼ teaspoon of grenadine. Shake in a vertical motion for 30 seconds. Strain slowly into a cocktail glass. Using a channel knife or standard vegetable peeler, gently slice only the skin (avoiding the bitter pith) of an orange above the drink and drop the peel into the glass.

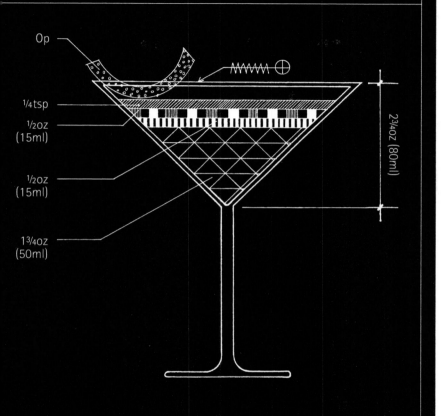

Op

¼tsp

½oz
(15ml)

½oz
(15ml)

1¾oz
(50ml)

2¾oz (80ml)

SPECIFICATIONS		EMBELLISHMENTS	
White rum	Orange curaçao	Orange peel (Op)	
Dry vermouth	Grenadine		

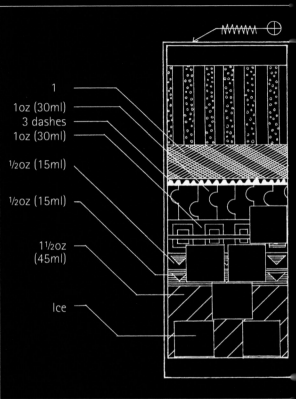

1

1oz (30ml)

3 dashes

1oz (30ml)

½oz (15ml)

½oz (15ml)

1½oz
(45ml)

Ice

SPECIFICATIONS

//// Gin	⊟⊟⊟ Simple syrup	
⋈⋈⋈ Fresh lemon juice	⊂⊂⊂⊂ Heavy cream	
⋈⋈⋈ Fresh lime juice	▼▼▼▼ Orange blossom wa

RAMOS GIN FIZZ

That the Ramos Gin Fizz has seen such resurgence across the cocktail-serving world is a little bit akin to the trend of reclaimed wood—why, in heaven's name, would you throw something so wonderful out the door? It's perfectly good material! And in the case of the Ramos Gin Fizz, the reclaimed materials have their origins in the southern United States' crescent-shaped city known as New Orleans—home to many a great tipple. The drink at hand was invented by namesake bartender Henry Ramos, whose refreshing concoction of gin, citrus, bubbles, cream, egg white, and orange blossom water combine to make maybe the loveliest of brunch-centric sippers in the civilized world. Really, though, you can drink it at any ol' time—but a hot day or night is definitely when you'll enjoy it best.

THE NOTES

Place 6 or 7 square ice cubes into a cocktail shaker. Pour in 1½ fluid ounces (45ml) of gin, coating the ice. Add in ½ fluid ounce (15ml) of fresh lemon juice, ½ fluid ounce (15ml) of fresh lime juice, 1 fluid ounce (30ml) of simple syrup (see p. 53), 1 fluid ounce (30ml) of heavy cream, 3 dashes of orange blossom water, and 1 egg white. Shake in a vertical motion for 30 seconds. Strain slowly into an ice-filled Collins glass. Top with club soda.

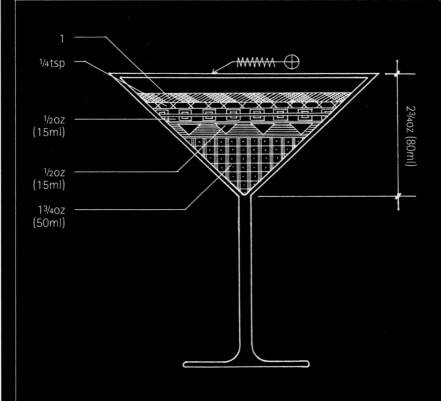

1

¼tsp

½oz
(15ml)

½oz
(15ml)

1¾oz
(50ml)

2¾oz (80ml)

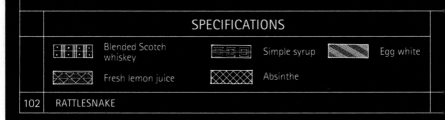

SPECIFICATIONS

Blended Scotch whiskey

Simple syrup

Egg white

Fresh lemon juice

Absinthe

RATTLESNAKE

A friend of mine from Texas once told me that, when he and his buddies go on hunting trips, it's not unusual to find pits of slithering rattlesnakes in the southwestern part of the state. The thought of it still gives me chills. I'm more aligned with the fictitious sentiment of Indiana Jones—"I hate snakes." But this is possibly the one snake I do like. Does it bite? A little. But it isn't poisonous (provided you don't overindulge). It's merely frisky. Its origins lay in the much-lingered-over pages of *The Savoy Cocktail Book*.

THE NOTES

Place 6 or 7 square ice cubes into a cocktail shaker. Pour in 1¾ fluid ounces (50ml) of blended Scotch whiskey, coating the ice. Add in ½ fluid ounce (15ml) of fresh lemon juice, ½ fluid ounce (15ml) of simple syrup, ¼ teaspoon of absinthe, and 1 egg white. Shake in a vertical motion for 30 seconds. Strain slowly into a cocktail glass.

ROBERT BURNS

The only thing certain about a Robert Burns (or "Bobby" or "Robbie," depending on who you are and where you come from) is that one of its never-wavering, always-constant materials is Scotch. Beyond that, well, the only other thing that is certain is that Robert Burns was a fine Scottish poet. Some say the Robert Burns contains absinthe; some say Bénédictine. Still others call for Drambuie with the stalwart pounding of a hearty walking stick. I like my Robert-Bobby-Robbie Burns—which, truly, is a twist on a Rob Roy; that's something it seems we can all agree upon—with a decent single malt (crazy, I know), Bénédictine, good sweet vermouth, and a dash of orange bitters.

THE NOTES

Place 6 or 7 square ice cubes into a cocktail shaker. Pour in 2 fluid ounces (60ml) of Scotch (a decent 12-year-old-single malt or blended, if you prefer), coating the ice. Add in ½ fluid ounce (15ml) of sweet vermouth, ¼ fluid ounce (8ml) of Bénédictine, and 1 dash of orange bitters. Shake in a vertical motion for 30 seconds. Strain slowly into a rocks glass.

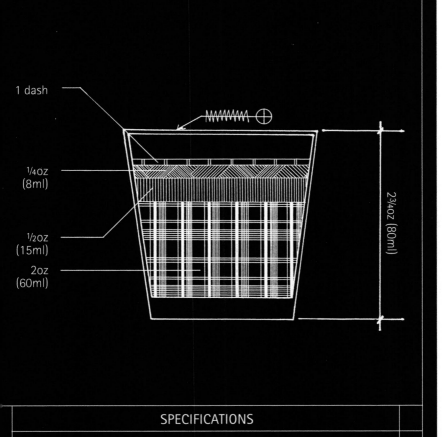

1 dash

¼oz
(8ml)

½oz
(15ml)

2oz
(60ml)

2¾oz (80ml)

SPECIFICATIONS

▦ Scotch		▨ Bénédictine	
▨ Sweet vermouth		▦ Orange bitters	

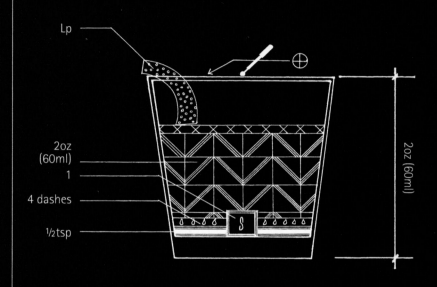

Lp

2oz
(60ml)

1

4 dashes

½tsp

2oz (60ml)

	SPECIFICATIONS		EMBELLISHMENTS
S	Sugar cube	Rye	
	Spring or purified water	Absinthe	Lemon peel (Lp)
Peychaud's Bitters			

SAZERAC

Created by famed Creole apothecary Antoine Peychaud in New Orleans,
Louisiana, during the early 19th century, today the Sazerac is the official
state-legislated cocktail of the Crescent City. Originally, the drink contained
cognac, a bit of water, a sugar cube, and Peychaud's very own namesake
bitters, but over the years the drink's ingredients morphed a bit. Grape-
based cognac became difficult to procure, due to a terrible little pest
called phylloxera that was rotting the vines of France. American-made
rye, however, was handy and a fortuitously delicious substitute. The then-
popular absinthe was added, giving the cocktail just a hint of an herbal
kick. Building this cocktail is an interesting exercise in the importance of
order of materials. You will need two rocks glasses; you will need to allow
one to chill and, after, patiently coat it with a swathe of absinthe. You will
then need to use the other for the important step of dissolving the sugar
and allowing the full marriage of the rye with it.

THE NOTES

Place 4 or 5 ice cubes into a rocks glass and set aside. Drop 1 sugar cube into a second rocks
glass. Drizzle with ½ teaspoon of spring or purified water and 4 dashes of Peychaud's Bitters.
Using a muddler or the back of a wooden spoon, muddle until the cube breaks apart and
dissolves. Add in 4 or 5 ice cubes and pour in 2 fluid ounces (60ml) of rye. Allow it to coat the
ice and stir. Discard the ice from the first glass and tilt on an angle. Drizzle in the absinthe
while slowly turning the glass clockwise, allowing the absinthe to completely coat the
inner sides of the glass. Strain the rye-sugar-bitters mix from the second glass into the first
absinthe-coated glass. Using a channel knife or standard vegetable peeler, gently slice only
the skin (avoiding the bitter pith) of a lemon above the drink and drop the peel into the glass.

SHERRY COBBLER

What's old is new, and that's what is so wonderful about the concept of the Sherry Cobbler, a popular, often wine-and-fruit-based 19th-century tipple, although, truly, the sky's the limit on your base ingredient here.

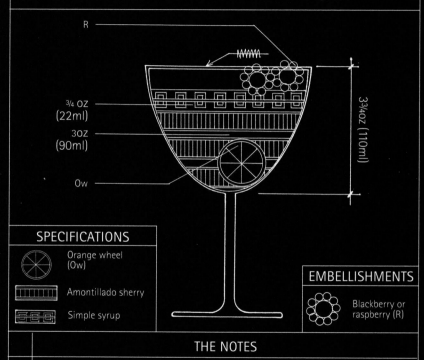

R

¾ OZ
(22ml)

3OZ
(90ml)

Ow

3¾oz (110ml)

SPECIFICATIONS

Orange wheel
(Ow)

Amontillado sherry

Simple syrup

EMBELLISHMENTS

Blackberry or
raspberry (R)

THE NOTES

Place 6 or 7 square ice cubes into a cocktail shaker. Slice an orange wheel into quarters and drop into the shaker. Pour in 3 fluid ounces (90ml) of amontillado sherry, coating the orange pieces and ice. Add in ¾ fluid ounce (22ml) of simple syrup (see p. 53). Shake in a vertical motion for 30 seconds. Pour, unstrained, into a wine glass. Garnish with 2 blackberries or raspberries.

SIDECAR

At your own home bar, this is one of the easiest bits of sipping sophistication you can craft. As long as you've got a lemon on hand and a decent orange liqueur (Cointreau is a good-quality, easy-to-find choice), you'll be sipping pretty in no time.

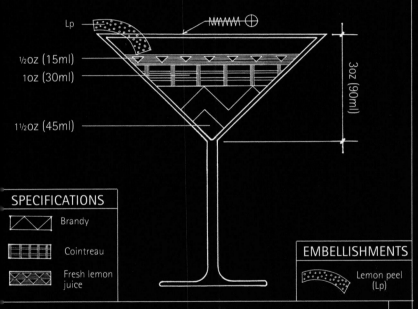

Lp

½oz (15ml)
1oz (30ml)

1½oz (45ml)

3oz (90ml)

SPECIFICATIONS

⬩ Brandy

⬩ Cointreau

⬩ Fresh lemon juice

EMBELLISHMENTS

Lemon peel (Lp)

THE NOTES

Place 6 or 7 square ice cubes into a cocktail shaker. Pour in 1½ fluid ounces (45ml) of brandy, coating the ice. Add in 1 fluid ounce (30ml) of Cointreau and ½ fluid ounce (15ml) of fresh lemon juice. Shake in a vertical motion for 30 seconds. Strain slowly into a cocktail glass. Using a channel knife or standard vegetable peeler, gently slice only the skin (avoiding the bitter pith) of a lemon above the drink and drop the peel into the glass.

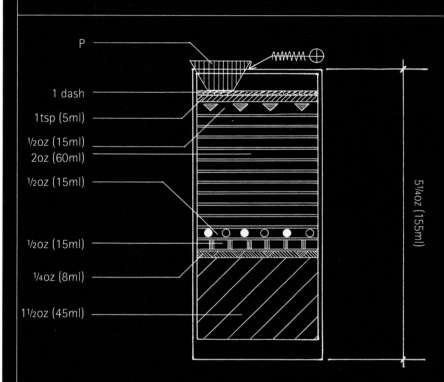

P

1 dash

1tsp (5ml)

½oz (15ml)

2oz (60ml)

½oz (15ml)

½oz (15ml)

¼oz (8ml)

1½oz (45ml)

5¼oz (155ml)

SPECIFICATIONS		EMBELLISHMENTS
Gin	Fresh pineapple juice	
Bénédictine	Fresh lime juice	
Cointreau	Grenadine	Pineapple wedge (P)
Cherry brandy	Angostura bitters	

SINGAPORE SLING

Kind of like prefabricated, cookie-cutter home trends, the Singapore Sling has suffered at the hands of bad materials and even worse memory recall. So much so that this delightful, heady, straw-sipping concoction more often than not resembles kicked-up Kool-Aid rather than the drink that was created at the Raffles Hotel in Singapore by bartender Ngiam Tong Boon. But this recipe, I promise, is the real deal: delicious, citrusy, sweet, and tart—just as it was originally intended.

THE NOTES

Place 6 or 7 square ice cubes into a cocktail shaker. Pour in 1½ fluid ounces (45ml) of gin, coating the ice. Add in ¼ fluid ounce (8ml) of Benedictine, ½ fluid ounce (15ml) of Cointreau, ½ fluid ounce (15ml) of cherry brandy, 2 fluid ounces (60ml) of fresh pineapple juice, ½ fluid ounce (15ml) of fresh lime juice, 1 teaspoon (5ml) of grenadine, and 1 dash of Angostura bitters. Shake in a vertical motion for 30 seconds. Strain slowly into a Collins glass. Garnish with a pineapple wedge.

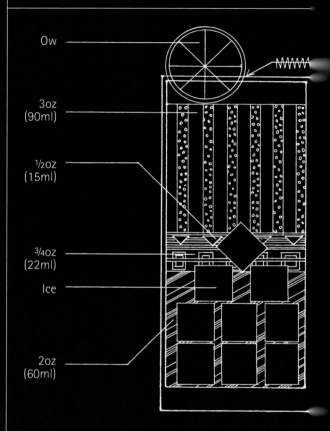

0w

3oz
(90ml)

1/2oz
(15ml)

3/4oz
(22ml)

Ice

2oz
(60ml)

SPECIFICATIONS

E

Sloe gin		Fresh lemon juice
Simple syrup		Club soda

SLOE GIN FIZZ

Sloe gin is an underused liqueur made from sloe berries, aka black-thorn, a form of wild plum native to Europe and Asia that grows like mad in the U.K. For a spell in America, it became kind of the Shirley Temple for grown-ups, all red in hue and loaded up with sticky-sweet maraschino cherries. Even worse, the type that was being imported was a saccharine form of the original, lacking entirely in a gin base. And then... It pretty much disappeared altogether in the States. Luckily, the good people at Plymouth rereleased the liqueur in its original form, and the Sloe Gin Fizz once again appeared on cocktail menus—only this time, it was the real deal.

THE NOTES

Place 6 or 7 square ice cubes into a cocktail shaker. Pour in 2 fluid ounces (60ml) of sloe gin, coating the ice. Add in ¾ fluid ounce (22ml) of simple syrup and ½ fluid ounce (15ml) of fresh lemon juice. Shake in a vertical motion for 30 seconds. Strain slowly into an ice-filled highball glass. Pour in 3 fluid ounces (90ml) of club soda. Garnish with an orange wheel.

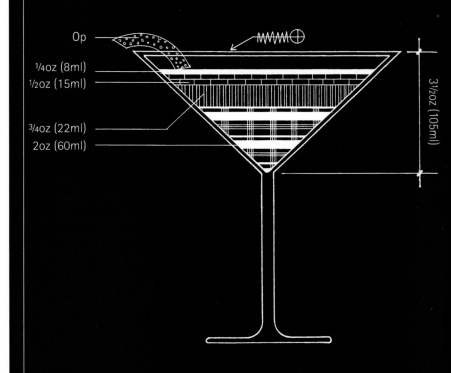

Op

1/4oz (8ml)
1/2oz (15ml)

3/4oz (22ml)
2oz (60ml)

3 1/2oz (105ml)

SPECIFICATIONS		EMBELLISHMENTS
Islay single-malt Scotch	Fresh orange juice	
Dry vermouth	Dubonnet Rouge	Orange peel (Op)

114   SOUL KISS

SOUL KISS

Balance might be one of the most important (and fleeting) concepts we deal with—in both life and cocktails. Tilt an ingredient a little too much this way or that and everything is out of whack. The Soul Kiss may well be the cocktail embodiment of the importance of this concept, mixing sweet and dry to balance the two just so. And then there's the choice of whiskey. Do you go a little on the sweet side with bourbon? Spicy with rye? Personally, I go a different route entirely. Unorthodox as it may sound, I love how a good, peaty Islay malt adds a gorgeous smoky edge to this pretty classic cocktail. If Islays aren't for you, pick your whiskey based on your own personal preference and let your palate be your guide.

THE NOTES

Place 6 or 7 square ice cubes into a cocktail shaker. Pour in 2 fluid ounces (60ml) of Islay single-malt Scotch, coating the ice. Add in ¾ fluid ounce (22ml) of dry vermouth, ½ fluid ounce (15ml) of fresh orange juice, and ¼ fluid ounce (8ml) of Dubonnet Rouge. Shake in a vertical motion for 30 seconds. Strain slowly into a cocktail glass. Using a channel knife or standard vegetable peeler, gently slice only the skin (avoiding the bitter pith) of an orange above the drink and drop the peel into the glass.

SOUTH SIDE

Since 1929, New York's "21" Club—its jockey statuettes standing sentry at the townhouse's West 52nd Street entrance—has remained one of Gotham's time-honored eating and drinking classics. It's only fitting that it has spawned a drink or two during its tenure—especially since the joint really began in myriad locales owned by enterprising cousins Jack Kreindler and Charlie Berns, who were known to have a speakeasy or three in their lifetimes.

THE NOTES

Place 6 or 7 square ice cubes into a cocktail shaker. Pour in 2 fluid ounces (60ml) of gin, coating the ice. Add in 1 fluid ounce (30ml) of fresh lemon juice, ½ fluid ounce (15ml) of simple syrup (see p.53), and 5 fresh mint leaves. Shake in a vertical motion for 30 seconds. Strain slowly into a Collins glass. Garnish with a mint sprig.

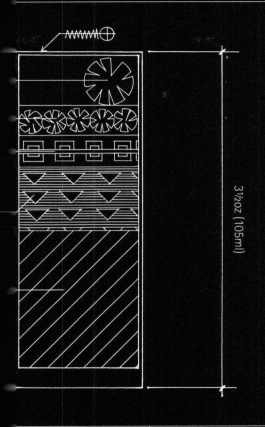

3½oz (105ml)

CATIONS

▦▦▦	Simple syrup	
⊛⊛⊛⊛	Mint	

EMBELLISHMENTS

✿	Mint sprig (Ms)

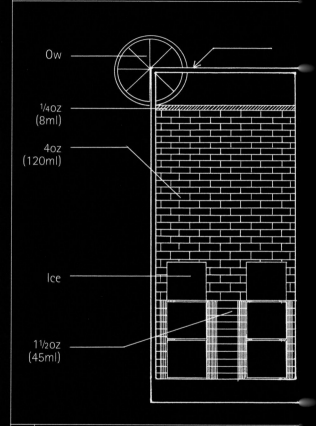

Ow

1/4oz
(8ml)

4oz
(120ml)

Ice

1 1/2oz
(45ml)

SPECIFICATIONS

▦	Silver tequila	▨	Grenadine
▦	Fresh orange juice		

TEQUILA SUNRISE

Have you ever seen a cross section of a building's foundation? The Tequila Sunrise is akin to this sort of "let's get a closer look at the bones" kind of examination—except far prettier and tastier and made semi-immortal in song by the Eagles. But if you're the type who likes to see the pieces at work, a Tequila Sunrise will be a rewarding drink for you. Each layer—orange, red, golden-hued, and, really, not too far off its name in terms of the evening sky in southerly climes—builds upon the next so that it's not just a lovely liquid vista to gaze upon but has layers of flavor to sip as well. Here more than ever it's vital not to substitute premade juice or low-quality grenadine in a pinch—make the effort to go for good-quality materials and you'll be handsomely rewarded with a delectable, sigh-inducing sipper.

THE NOTES

Place 5 or 6 square ice cubes into a highball glass. Pour in 1½ fluid ounces (45ml) of silver tequila coating the ice and allowing it to settle. Slowly add in 4 fluid ounces (120ml) of fresh orange juice. Using the back of a spoon, slowly drizzle in ¼ fluid ounce (8ml) of grenadine. Garnish with an orange wheel.

TOM COLLINS

The Tom Collins falls into the sours category of drinks—a refreshing aid meant for hot, summery days lounging around the pool
or firing up the barbecue in the backyard. When imparting the
sour side of things into a cocktail, don't take shortcuts. In the
end, they're not that short, as they require you to plunk down
cash on unnecessary and poorly made materials that will crumble
the foundation of your cocktail faster than you can say, "Check,
please!" Having citrus fruit on hand is easy enough and cheaper
most of the time. The Collins range of drinks is wonderfully inter-
changeable with myriad spirits—whiskey, vodka, tequila, brandy—
all make perfectly lovely versions of the drink, so if gin isn't your
foundation of choice, feel free to resketch the blueprint to match
your own tastes. The Tom Collins, though, is a gin classic and a
favorite, as much for its refreshing spritz of citrus as for its herby,
bright base spirit's complementary flavors.

THE NOTES

Place 6 or 7 square ice cubes into a cocktail shaker. Pour in 1¾ fluid ounces (50ml) of gin,
coating the ice. Add in ¾ fluid ounce (22ml) of simple syrup (see p.53) and ½ fluid ounce
(15ml) of fresh lemon juice. Shake in a vertical motion for 30 seconds. Strain slowly into an
ice-filled Collins glass. Top with club soda. Garnish with a lemon wedge.

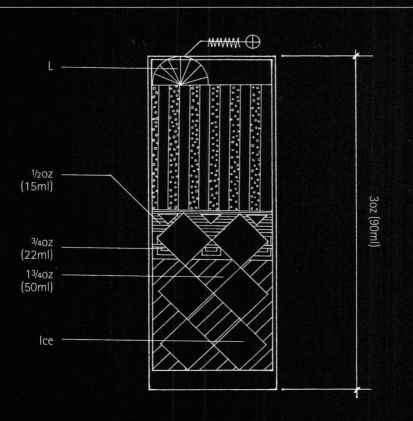

L

1/2OZ
(15ml)

3/4OZ
(22ml)

13/4OZ
(50ml)

Ice

3oz (90ml)

SPECIFICATIONS		EMBELLISHMENTS	
Gin	Fresh lemon juice	Lemon wedge (L)	
Simple syrup	Club soda		

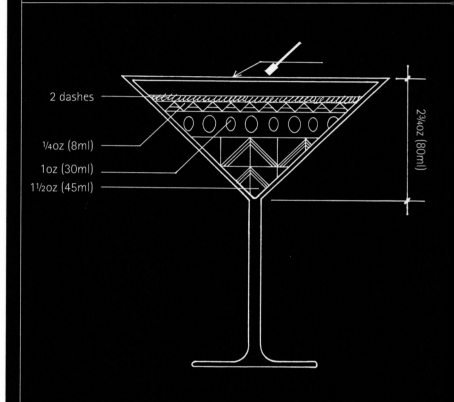

2 dashes

¼oz (8ml)

1oz (30ml)

1½oz (45ml)

2¾oz (80ml)

SPECIFICATIONS

Rye

Grand Marnier

Manzanilla sherry

Angostura bitters

UP-TO-DATE

Calling something "up-to-date" is always a risky proposition. Sunken living rooms and beanbag chairs were super up-to-date at one time; A-frame houses were all the rage once upon a time; and remember Tuscan-inspired interiors? Yeah, that was big, too. What's here today is gone tomorrow, but that's what's so cool about classics. But even classics aren't completely immune to the whims of trend and can fall out of favor. The Up-to-Date has gotten a little dusting off in the 21st century, thanks to the wholehearted embrace of whiskies and, more recently, sherry among the drinking cognoscenti. It's a super-sophisticated tipple that's more to the savory side of sipping than sweet.

THE NOTES

Place 6 or 7 square ice cubes into a cocktail shaker. Pour in 1½ fluid ounces (45ml) of rye, coating the ice. Add in 1 fluid ounce (30ml) of Manzanilla sherry, ¼ fluid ounce (8ml) of Grand Marnier, and 2 dashes of Angostura bitters. Using a long bar spoon, stir for 20 seconds. Strain slowly into a cocktail glass.

VANDERBILT

When something works well, it's not inappropriate at all to mimic or build upon those initial well-drawn plans. That's what I think about with this drink. In some ways, the Vanderbilt reminds me a lot of the Manhattan: the two-to-one measurement of the main spirit ingredients; the dark side of spirits influenced with a bit of cherry and a bit of sweetness. And, yet, the Vanderbilt is its own concoction entirely. I like to add an orange peel to this drink because I think it complements both the brandies nicely.

THE NOTES

Place 6 or 7 square ice cubes into a cocktail shaker. Pour in 2 fluid ounces (60ml) of brandy, coating the ice. Add in 1 fluid ounce (30ml) of cherry brandy, ¼ fluid ounce (8ml) of simple syrup (see p.53), and 2 dashes of Angostura bitters. Using a long bar spoon, stir for 20 seconds. Strain slowly into a cocktail glass. Using a channel knife or standard vegetable peeler, gently slice only the skin (avoiding the bitter pith) of an orange above the drink and drop the peel into the glass.

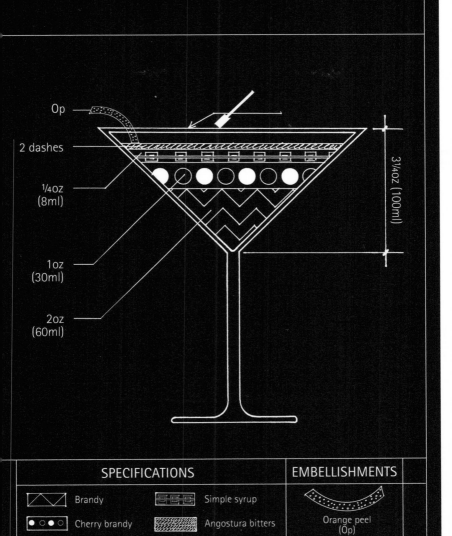

Op

2 dashes

1/4oz
(8ml)

1oz
(30ml)

2oz
(60ml)

3 1/4oz (100ml)

SPECIFICATIONS

Brandy

Cherry brandy

Simple syrup

Angostura bitters

EMBELLISHMENTS

Orange peel
(Op)

VENETIAN SPRITZ

Sparkling wine is like an elevator in a glass, taking aromas and flavors and shooting them to the top, adding a great bit of buoyancy to the body of a drink. The Venetian Spritz is best made with prosecco, as that mix of fruit-forward sparkling wine with bitter, herby Aperol makes for a really refreshing combination. This is such a great, easy aperitif or party drink to kick off an evening in an incredibly festive and colorful way.

THE NOTES

Place 4 or 5 ices cubes into a rocks glass. Pour in 3 fluid ounces (90ml) of prosecco, 1 fluid ounce (30ml) of Aperol, and top with club soda. Garnish with an orange slice.

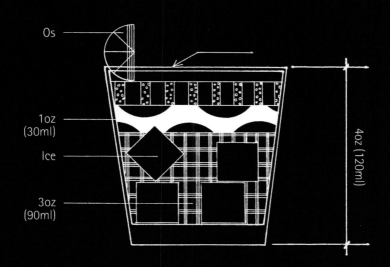

Os

1oz
(30ml)

Ice

3oz
(90ml)

4oz (120ml)

SPECIFICATIONS

Prosecco   Club soda

Aperol

EMBELLISHMENTS

Orange slice
(Os)

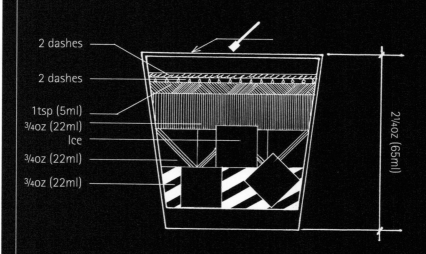

2 dashes

2 dashes

1tsp (5ml)

3/4oz (22ml)

Ice

3/4oz (22ml)

3/4oz (22ml)

2¼oz (65ml)

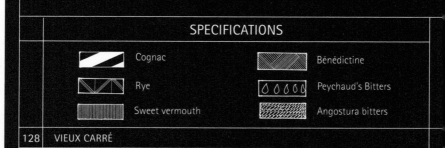

SPECIFICATIONS

Cognac		Bénédictine
Rye		Peychaud's Bitters
Sweet vermouth		Angostura bitters

VIEUX CARRÉ

In the fair city of New Orleans there are many, many wonderful architectural elements that seem at once old and classic and yet utterly unique to NOLA itself. What might be one of the more oddball elements can be found in the bar of the lovely Hotel Monteleone. It is there that an actual antique carousel was fashioned into a bar and spins (slowly—you can imagine what fast-moving spinning motions combined with alcohol might do to a person...). Their signature cocktail—the Vieux Carré—is the Gallic term for the famed neighborhood in which the Carousel Bar takes its happy customers for a ride every day, the French Quarter.

THE NOTES

Place 6 or 7 square ice cubes into a cocktail shaker. Pour in ¾ fluid ounce (22ml) of cognac, coating the ice. Add in ¾ fluid ounce (22ml) of rye, ¾ fluid ounce (22ml) of sweet vermouth, 1 teaspoon (5ml) of Bénédictine, and 2 dashes each of both Peychaud's and Angostura bitters. Using a long bar spoon, stir for 20 seconds. Strain slowly into an ice-filled rocks glass.

WHISKEY SANGAREE

Sangarees are wonderfully simple cocktails to build and yet simultaneously offer up both complexity and the ability to refresh—a pretty neat trick. In some ways, they have echoes of mulled wine, with the additions of both port and freshly grated nutmeg, but then they go in an entirely different direction as cocktails that are not only served cold but also use just one glass in the making. Just add (sparkling) water and, presto—your sangaree is ready.

THE NOTES

Place 3 or 4 ice cubes into a rocks glass. Pour in 2 fluid ounces (60ml) of bourbon, ½ fluid ounce (15ml) of ruby port, and ¼ fluid ounce (8ml) of simple syrup (see p.53). Using a bar spoon, stir for about 10 seconds. Top with club soda. Garnish with freshly grated nutmeg.

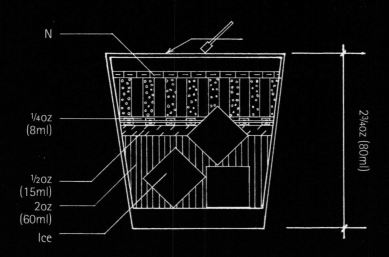

N

1/4 OZ
(8ml)

1/2 OZ
(15ml)

2 OZ
(60ml)

Ice

2¾oz (80ml)

WHISKEY SOUR

The idea of the sour—a drink that offers the puckery tartness of lemon citrus combined with just enough of a sweet element to keep it from going over the edge into sour territory—is to be refreshing. And while you can make it with pretty much any base spirit you like—whiskey, gin, brandy, vodka, tequila—there's something really great about the combination of vanilla-influenced bourbon with a sour element, reminiscent of SweeTart candies that you may remember from being a kid (just, you know, in a much better, grown-up way…).

THE NOTES

Place 6 or 7 square ice cubes into a cocktail shaker. Pour in 2 fluid ounces (60ml) of bourbon, coating the ice. Add in 1 fluid ounce (30ml) of fresh lemon juice and 3/4 fluid ounce (22ml) of simple syrup. Shake in a vertical motion for 30 seconds. Strain slowly into an ice-filled rocks glass. Garnish with a brandied cherry.

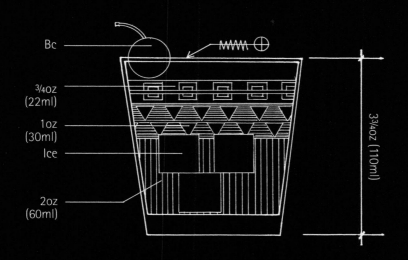

Bc

3/4oz
(22ml)

1oz
(30ml)

Ice

2oz
(60ml)

3¾oz (110ml)

SPECIFICATIONS			EMBELLISHMENTS	
Bourbon		Simple syrup		
Fresh lemon juice			Brandied cherry (Bc)	

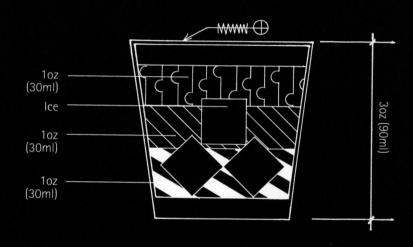

1oz
(30ml)

Ice

1oz
(30ml)

1oz
(30ml)

3oz (90ml)

SPECIFICATIONS

Kahlúa		Cream	
Vodka			

WHITE RUSSIAN

WHITE RUSSIAN

With two heavy and one lighter ingredient in a White Russian, you can go a couple of ways in creating it. One methodology is to treat each material like a layer to build upon—dark, rich coffee liqueur at the bottom; cool, chilly vodka in the middle and a float of cream on top. The second method is my preferred style of building this drink, though: shaken mightily so that the three combine and the cream becomes frothy. I believe that, together, the sum of their parts becomes a far more memorable textural and flavor experience.

THE NOTES

Place 6 or 7 square ice cubes into a cocktail shaker. Pour in 1 fluid ounce (30ml) of Kahlúa, coating the ice. Add in 1 fluid ounce (30ml) of vodka and 1 fluid ounce (30ml) of cream. Shake in a vertical motion for 30 seconds. Strain slowly into an ice-filled rocks glass.

WIDOW'S KISS

Dangerous to drink? Maybe—but not in the life-threatening way the name implies. The Widow's Kiss is sort of an outdoorsy cocktail in the sense that its ingredients may make you think of a walk in the country. There's the apple of the calvados and then the herby bite of the Chartreuse, Bénédictine, and bitters. It's the best kind of spring cocktail—the one that's kind of akin to that first time you throw open the windows after a long winter indoors and take a deep breath. Smell not the hint of demise that the name brings to mind but the promise of new things growing.

THE NOTES

Place 6 or 7 square ice cubes into a cocktail shaker. Pour in 1½ fluid ounces (45ml) of calvados, coating the ice. Add in ½ fluid ounce (15ml) of green Chartreuse, ½ fluid ounce (15ml) of Bénédictine, and 2 dashes of Angostura bitters. Shake in a vertical motion for 30 seconds. Strain slowly into a cocktail glass. Garnish with a brandied cherry.

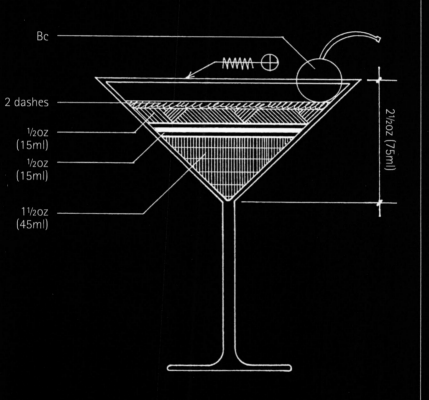

Bc

2 dashes

1/2oz
(15ml)

1/2oz
(15ml)

1 1/2oz
(45ml)

2 1/2oz (75ml)

SPECIFICATIONS		EMBELLISHMENTS	
Calvados	Bénédictine	Brandied cherry (Bc)	
Green Chartreuse	Angostura bitters		

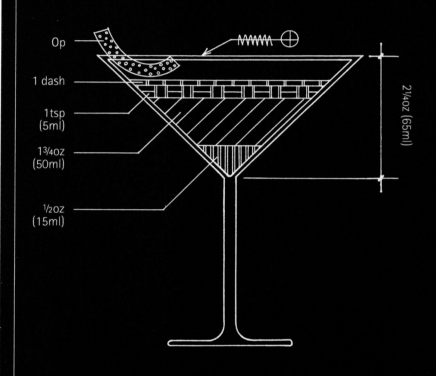

Op

1 dash

1tsp
(5ml)

1¾oz
(50ml)

½oz
(15ml)

2¼oz (65ml)

	SPECIFICATIONS		EMBELLISHMENTS
▥ Dry vermouth	▦ Blue curaçao		Orange peel (Op)
▨ Gin	▤ Orange bitters		

YALE

No need for alumnus status to enjoy this blue-hued sipper—a love of gin and oranges will do just fine. There is evidence pointing to the earliest incarnation of this drink eschewing the blue curaçao that gives the Yale its school-colors hue (not to mention that orange influence), but for the sake of a visual cue, I think it's fun to leave it in.

THE NOTES

Place 6 or 7 square ice cubes into a cocktail shaker. Pour in ½ fluid ounce (15ml) of dry vermouth, coating the ice. Add in 1¾ fluid ounces (50ml) of gin, 1 teaspoon (5ml) of blue curaçao, and 1 dash of orange bitters. Shake in a vertical motion for 30 seconds. Strain slowly into a cocktail glass. Using a channel knife or standard vegetable peeler, gently slice only the skin (avoiding the bitter pith) of an orange and drop the peel into the glass.

ZOMBIE

The Zombie—umbrella garnish and all—may well be the mack daddy of all tiki drinks, with its multitude of fruit juices and abundance of tropical-style garnishes, all Sears Tower-tall and ready for your straw-sipping pleasure. And, really, it may well make you as dizzy as the view from such heights with its heady mix of rums, brandy, and orange curaçao. Created by famed bartender Donn Beach, the Zombie actually debuted to its biggest audience at the 1939 World's Fair.

THE NOTES

Place 6 or 7 square ice cubes into a cocktail shaker. Pour in 1¼ fluid ounces (40ml) of dark spiced rum, coating the ice. Add in 1¼ fluid ounces (40ml) of white rum, ½ fluid ounce (15ml) of orange curaçao, ½ fluid ounce (15ml) of fresh lemon juice, ½ fluid ounce (15ml) of fresh lime juice, ½ fluid ounce (15ml) of fresh pink grapefruit juice, ¾ fluid ounce (22ml) of fresh pineapple juice, ¼ fluid ounce (8ml) of grenadine, and 2 dashes of Angostura bitters. Shake in a vertical motion for 30 seconds. Strain slowly into an ice-filled Collins glass. Garnish with a pineapple wedge and a paper umbrella.

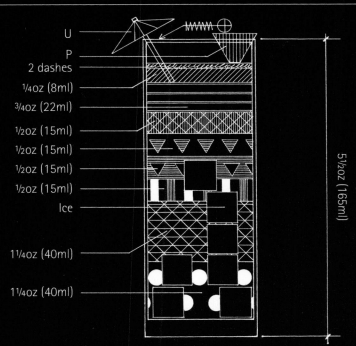

U
P
2 dashes
¼oz (8ml)
¾oz (22ml)
½oz (15ml)
½oz (15ml)
½oz (15ml)
½oz (15ml)
Ice
1¼oz (40ml)
1¼oz (40ml)

5½oz (165ml)

SPECIFICATIONS

●●● Dark rum		▨▨▨ Fresh grapefruit juice (pink)	
⨯⨯⨯ White rum		▬▬▬ Fresh pineapple juice	
▮▮▮ Orange curaçao		▨▨ Grenadine	
⨯⨯⨯ Fresh lemon juice		▨▨▨ Angostura bitters	
▽▽▽ Fresh lime juice			

EMBELLISHMENTS

Pineapple wedge (P)

Paper umbrella (U)

FRAMING YOUR COCKTAILS

I've often heard this question posed: "Does it *really* matter what glass I put my drink in?" Yes, it does. The glass you use is in large part the frame of reference for how much liquid will be in your drink. Some cocktails require less space; some require more. And the fact is, you can't fit a Whiskey Collins into a cocktail glass, and you would be sorely disappointed to see a Cosmo in a hurricane glass. Also, keep in mind that it's not just about whether there are cubes in your glass or not—at some point, your mixable will likely touch ice—an important factor, as the requisite dilution from it is a necessary consideration for any drink. Ever try a martini that wasn't stirred or shaken with ice? Youch! That bit of water that mixes with your gin and vermouth isn't just something that happens; it's absolutely necessary. And so is the space in which you eventually sip it. What follows is a simple rundown of the glassware used for the cocktails presented on these pages. They are by no means exhaustive, but they will get you correctly mixing each and every drink here, not to mention an entire library of others.

CHAMPAGNE FLUTE

6–8 ounces. Long, slim, and elegant, an impercep-tible bit of etching at the bottom of the flute is what helps the bubbles make their merry, fast float to the brim of the glass.

COCKTAIL AND COUPE GLASSES

4–10 ounces. Typically used for shaken or stirred drinks that are not served over ice and strained, the difference between the two is truly one of aesthetics. The cock-tail glass, shaped in a sleek "V", and the coupe—a round-bottomed, old-fashioned champagne glass.

STEMWARE

COLLINS GLASS

12–14 ounces. Myriad Collins drinks are the obvious shoo-in for this tall, ample glass, but it's also often used for mixables that contain a bevy of juices and/or sodas, as well as a good option for tropical concoctions like the Mai Tai.

HIGHBALL GLASS

10–12 ounces. The right choice for simple two-note drinks that go over ice—like a bourbon and ginger ale or a gin and tonic.

HURRICANE GLASS

14–18 ounces. Its namesake cocktail and its many ingredients fit nicely into its curvy shape, but the hurricane also works well for frozen drinks or even Bloody Marys, if you're so inclined.

PORT GLASS

4–8 ounces. I always find port glasses to be more versatile than they're given credit—for after-dinner sipping, as well as for layered concoctions.

PUNCH CUP

6–8 ounces. There's nothing more elegant and fun than demure-ly sipping punch from its requisite broad-rimmed cup. Great for everything from wintery eggnog to refreshing summer sippers to warmed mulled cider.

ROCKS GLASS

5–8 ounces. Short and stocky, the rocks glass is the workhorse of any bar. Fill it with ice and the sky's the limit, from a Sazerac to a Martini on the rocks.

WINEGLASS

10–16 ounces. Another often overlooked glass, the wineglass isn't just for vino anymore. Use it as an elegant presentation for frothy milk-based drinks; a prettier presentation for cocktails on the rocks; and it also makes a good foundation for a Bloody Mary.

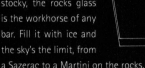

For Dad and his diligence.
For Mom and her martinis.
MW

ABOUT THE AUTHOR/ILLUSTRATOR

AMY ZAVATTO writes about spirits, cocktails, wine, and other potables in New York City. She's a contributing editor to *Imbibe* magazine and holds a Level III Certificate from the Wine & Spirit Education Trust. Her favorite drink is a Manhattan.

MELISSA WOOD is an illustrator, designer, and architectural aficionada who pored over Charles Addams' and James Thurber's cartoons as a child and dreamed of one day illustrating a book of her own. Melissa has three terrific children and makes a wicked Bloody Mary.

EMBELLISHMENTS

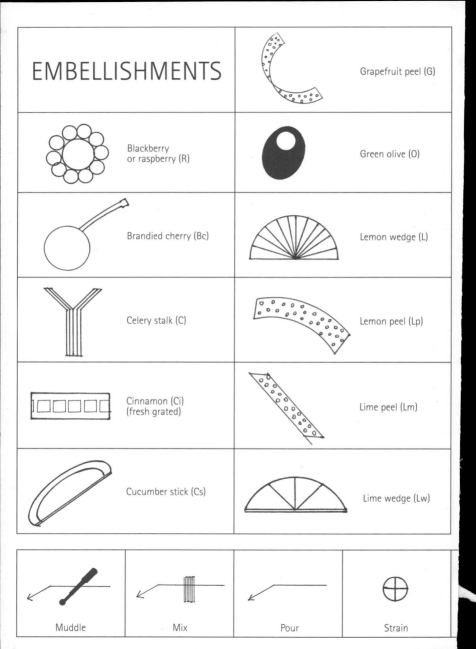

	Grapefruit peel (G)
Blackberry or raspberry (R)	Green olive (O)
Brandied cherry (Bc)	Lemon wedge (L)
Celery stalk (C)	Lemon peel (Lp)
Cinnamon (Ci) (fresh grated)	Lime peel (Lm)
Cucumber stick (Cs)	Lime wedge (Lw)

Muddle	Mix	Pour	Strain